The Selfishness
of Others

The Selfishness of Others

•

An Essay on
the Fear of Narcissism

Kristin Dombek

Farrar, Straus and Giroux   New York

Farrar, Straus and Giroux
18 West 18th Street, New York 10011

The "Diagnostic Criteria for Narcissistic Personality Disorder" is reprinted with
permission from the *Diagnostic and Statistical Manual of Mental Disorders*,
Fifth Edition (copyright 2013). American Psychiatric Association.

Library of Congress Cataloging-in-Publication Data
Names: Dombek, Kristin, [date] author.
Title: The selfishness of others : an essay on the fear of narcissism / Kristin
    Dombek.
Description: First Edition. | New York, NY : FSG Originals, 2016. | Includes
    bibliographical references.
Identifiers: LCCN 2015048669 | ISBN 9780865478237 (paperback) |
    ISBN 9780374712549 (e-book)
Subjects: LCSH: Narcissism. | Interpersonal relations. | BISAC: SOCIAL
    SCIENCE / Essays. | PSYCHOLOGY / Personality. | PSYCHOLOGY /
    Interpersonal Relations.
Classification: LCC BF575.N35 D56 2016 | DDC 155.2/32—dc23
LC record available at http://lccn.loc.gov/2015048669

Designed by Jonathan D. Lippincott

Our books may be purchased in bulk for promotional, educational, or
business use. Please contact your local bookseller or the
Macmillan Corporate and Premium Sales Department at
1-800-221-7945, extension 5442, or by e-mail at
MacmillanSpecialMarkets@macmillan.com.

www.fsgbooks.com • www.fsgoriginals.com
www.twitter.com/fsgbooks • www.facebook.com/fsgbooks

1   3   5   7   9   10   8   6   4   2

*Note to readers: Some identifying details and dialogue, as well as the language
of some Internet posts, have been changed.*

I'll bet you think this song is about you.

—Carly Simon

Contents

The Cold   3

The Epidemic   17

The Bad Boyfriend   31

The Millennial   61

The Murderer   89

The Artist   111

The World   121

Notes   *139*

Selected Bibliography   *145*

Acknowledgments   *149*

The Selfishness
of Others

The Cold

We know the new selfishness when we see it. It's in the laughter of the Atlanta girl who demanded the city's busiest avenue be shut down for her arrival to her sixteenth birthday party, even though there was a hospital across the street. It's in the way that, when the party planner pointed out the traffic, she said, "My sweet sixteen is more important than wherever they have to be," and when he pointed out the hospital, she giggled and said that the ambulances could just "go around." It's in the way she didn't give a shit about the sick and dying but did give very much of a shit when, in a store a few minutes after talking to the party planner, she was offered ugly dresses to try on, because why would she even go to her own party if she didn't look hotter than everyone else? It's in the way she not only did all this but did it shamelessly, on camera, for MTV's reality television show *My Super Sweet 16*, and how, when it comes to millennials, this is just everything.

It's in the smile on the face of the professional bad

boyfriend, whose website led with "I'm an asshole" next to a picture of him with his arm around a woman with her face blanked out and "Your face here" printed across the blank, an image from the cover of one of the books about getting wasted and sportfucking that earned him celebrity, a small fortune, and hero status in a movement among men to obtain power over women by insulting them and regularly withdrawing or disappearing, and who also happens to have been born in Atlanta, which may or may not be important. It's in the way it's getting harder to remember if there was a time before being a manipulative, shallow, grandiose asshole was something to brag about, before people shopped and exchanged one another like accessories to a personal brand.

And at its most horrifying, it's in the smile on the face of the murderer. The one who set off a van bomb in a government quarter, killing eight people, and then went to an island where teenagers were at summer camp and slaughtered sixty-nine of them as they tried to run and swim away, and who, when he was arrested and photographed, smirked contentedly. The one who, when asked if he had any empathy for his victims and their families, spoke not of their suffering but of his, of how traumatic it was for him to see all that blood, who complained about a cut on his finger and said he did it all to market his manifesto—more than fifteen hundred pages long—against women and Muslims, a manifesto that, like his Facebook page, featured pictures of him smiling in Knights Templar costumes. It's in the photos and wounded rants that all the murderers now post on Facebook before they walk into schools and movie theaters with guns, as if a moment's celebrity is worth any human life, even their own.

In the laughter, the smiles, the rants, and the violence we see a coldness, an absence of empathy rivaled only by a terrible need for attention. This is a kind of selfishness we increasingly fear, judging by the rising chorus that calls the young and the bad boyfriends by the same name as the murderers: narcissist.

But what is wrong with the narcissist? This is harder to know. If you see the smile on the face of a murderer, you must run. But if you are unlucky enough to love someone who seems suddenly so into himself that he doesn't care who he hurts, someone who turns from warm to gone when he doesn't need you, so self-adoring or wounded he meets criticism with violence or icy rage, who turns into another person in front of your eyes, or simply turns away when he said he'd be there—if you love someone who seems to have the particular twenty-first-century selfishness in some more subtle or, worse, invisible way, you will likely go to the Internet for help. There, you'll be told that, yes, your loved one has the same disorder as the murderers, a new selfishness different in scope but not in quality from those characters who are the very incarnation of what we mean when we say *evil*. You'll read, in that sizable portion of the self-help Internet we might call, awkwardly, the narcisphere, a story that can change the way you see everything, if you start believing in it, giving you the uncanny but slightly exciting sensation that you're living in a movie. It's familiar, this movie, as if you've seen it before, and it's a creepy one, but you have the most important role in the script. You're the hero, and the movie goes, more or less, like this.

•

At first, the narcissist is extraordinarily charming, even kind and sweet. Then, after a while, he seems full of himself. It could be a "he" or a "she," but let's stick with "he." That's what you start to think, when you know someone like this: he's full of himself. But the narcissist is empty.

Normal, healthy people are full of self, a kind of substance like a soul or personhood that, if you have it, emanates warmly from inside of you toward the outside of you. No one knows what it is, but everyone agrees that narcissists do not have it. Disturbingly, however, they are often better than anyone else at seeming to have it. Because what they have inside is empty space, they have had to make a study of the selves of others in order to invent something that looks and sounds like one. Narcissists are imitators par excellence. The murderer plagiarized most of his manifesto, obviously and badly, but often narcissists are so good at imitating that you won't even notice. And they do not copy the small, boring parts of selves. They take what they think are the biggest, most impressive parts of other selves, and devise a hologram of self that seems superpowered. Let's call it "selfiness," this simulacrum of a superpowered self. Sometimes they seem crazy or are really dull, but often, perhaps because they have had to try harder than most to make it, the selfiness they've come up with is qualitatively better, when you first encounter it, than the ordinary, naturally occurring selves of normal, healthy people. Narcissists are the most popular kids at school. They are rock stars. They are movie stars. They are not all really rock stars or movie stars, but they seem like they are. They may tell you that you are the only one who really sees them for who they really are, which is probably a trick. If one of your parents is a narcissist, he or she will tell you that you are a rock star, too, which is definitely a trick.

Because for the narcissist, this appreciation of you is entirely contingent on the idea that you will help him to maintain his selfiness. If you do not, or if you are near him when someone or something does not, then God help you. When that picture shatters, his hurt and his rage will be unmatched in its heat or, more often, its coldness. He will unfriend you, stop following you, stop returning your emails, stop talking to you completely. He will cheat on you without seeming to think it's a big deal, or break up with you, when he has said he'd be with you forever. He will fire you casually and without notice. Whatever hurts most, he will do it. Whatever you need the most, he will withhold it. He cannot feel other people's feelings, but he is uncannily good at figuring out how to demolish yours. When this happens, your pain will be the pain of finding out that you have held the most wrong belief that you've ever been stupid enough to hold: the belief that because this asshole loved you, the world could be better than usual, better than it is for everyone else.

It isn't that the narcissist is just not a good person; she's like a caricature of what we mean by "not a good person." She's not just bad; she's a living, breathing lesson in what badness is. Take Immanuel Kant's elegant formulation of how to do the right thing: act in ways that could be generalized to universal principles. You'll choose the right thing to do, every time, if you ask yourself: If everyone acted in this way, would the world be a better place? Reason will always guide you to the right answer, and to its corollary, which is that we should treat others never as means but always as ends in themselves. The narcissist, in contrast, always chooses to act in exactly such a way that if everyone were to follow suit, the world would go straight to hell.

It might take you a while to realize that the narcissist is not merely selfish, but doesn't actually have a self. When you do, it will seem spooky, how good she has been at performing something you thought was care. Now you see that she is like a puppet, a clown, an animate corpse, anything that looks human but isn't. For the narcissist, life is only a stage, writes Alexander Lowen, the author of *Narcissism: Denial of the True Self*, quoted on the Wikipedia page about narcissism, and "when the curtain falls upon an act, it is finished and forgotten. The emptiness of such a life is beyond imagination." You might empathize: how horrible to live this way, having to imitate self-ness all the time. You can think of it that way, compassionately—intimacy issues, attachment styles, some childhood trauma beyond their control—or you can decide that your compassion is another sign you've been tricked: that because the narcissist has a priori no empathy, yours is just applause to her, and she is not just fake, but evil.

If you work for a narcissist, or are the child of one, or are in love with one, what should you do? Some mental health professionals think that you can love a narcissist, in a way, but that you just have to treat him or her like a six-year-old and expect nothing from that person. Some do think that narcissists can change. Deciding between these two theories can haunt you forever. And on the Internet, the change theory is a minority opinion; just about everyone advises that if a narcissist begins to entangle you, you should run. As one blogger put it: "What does one do when encountering a narcissist for the first time? The simple answer: grab your running shoes and start your first 5K right there in the middle of the cocktail party!"

Something that might bother you, if you know someone who you think may have the new selfishness, and pause to consider the narcissism story's logical claims, is this: If he is empty inside, this narcissist, who or what is it, inside of him, that is imitating having a self? If he is nothing but a performance, who or what is doing the performing? Is he animating his selfness with another, also fake, part of his selfness? But what, then, is animating that part? If the descriptions of narcissism sometimes don't exactly make sense, in this way, how can they describe so creepily well most ex-boyfriends and so many bosses? Why is having a boyfriend or a boss so much like having your own personal villain, anyway? If the uncannily accurate descriptions of your personal villain imply that he or she is outside the empire of normal mental health, flickering eerily at the edge of pathology, having the same disorder, or at least traits of the same disorder, as a man who would chase children across an island and murder every one he can catch, why do these descriptions also (in moments you quietly bury deep inside you) remind you, sometimes, of an entirely different person—that is, you? And why does the nightmare described by the Internet, of encountering people who look and sound real but are fake, remind you so much of the feeling of reading the Internet itself?

There isn't time for these questions, according to the narcissism script; there isn't time to do anything but put on your running shoes and embark upon your first 5K. It will likely not be your last. In this day and age, you will have to run that distance again and again. Because the story about the new selfishness is not just about your boyfriend or even the millennials or the murderers. According to Neil J. Lavender, a *Psychology Today* blogger and co-author of the books *The One*-Way *Relationship Handbook*, *Impossible to Please*, and *Toxic Coworkers*, "Like so many mental health professionals we believe that there are more narcissists today living in the United States than at any other time, with the millennial generation leading the pack. Our entitlement, rock star, 'all about me' mentality seems to be a swamp for breeding narcissists." And a few clicks away are hundreds of blogs and articles and features and books that say the very same thing, that there is an epidemic of narcissism that started in the United States but is spreading fast, that even Europeans are becoming more selfish and that in China, where the disorder is compounded by the "Little Emperor" syndrome caused by the one-child policy, the millennials might be even more self-obsessed than ours—that we live in a time so rampant with narcissisms, so flush with false selves masquerading as real selves so selfish that they feed on other selves, a time so full of contagious emptiness, that ours is a moment in history that is, more than any other, absolutely exceptional.

•

It's winter in the northeastern United States, and cold. Something called a "polar vortex" is hovering north of the country. There has been blizzard after blizzard. The storms are named after gods, and they come in alphabetical order, like hurricanes: Atlas, Boreus, Cleon, Deon, Electra. In Chicago and Minneapolis, it feels like −30 degrees Fahrenheit. The movie *Frozen* is the winter blockbuster, and the hit song is "Let It Go," sung by a princess who's turned her kingdom to ice, making it seem as if the weather were part of a Disney marketing campaign. The app is Tinder, *selfie* has been declared the word of the year, and a study has come out showing that our language is more self-centered than ever before. You can see it in song lyrics, in novels, and in nonfiction. American writers are using *I* and *me* 42 percent more than they did in 1960. Making its way around the Internet is a picture of Obama with the caption "Obama uses 'I' and 'Me' 117 times in one speech while walking on water." The literary establishment has read the first two volumes of a 3,500-page, six-part autobiographical novel about every mundane detail of the life of a sweet but anxious and self-absorbed Norwegian man. It's a winter when it's easy enough to find oneself hunched over one's computer screen, locked in horrified gaze at the self-adoration of others, and look up to find one's friends talking on and on about themselves, their words frozen and repeating "I," "I," "I." Listening to them, wondering if they even remember you exist, is like watching Narcissus bent over that still pool in Ovid's myth, stuck in the inaugural selfie.

If more and more people are now more evil and fake, using the rest of us only as means to fill their contagious emptiness, Kant's elegant formulation no longer works; it assumes that because reason is our guide, others will, for the most part, act in the ways they wish everyone else to act. But that is not the worst of it; the recommended treatment for an individual narcissist—give up, run—doesn't scale, either. If narcissists are increasing in number, and everyone were to run a 5K from everyone else all the time, there would be serious logistical issues. But setting these aside, the strategy enacts the very coldness described by the diagnosis, as if the only way to escape the emptiness contagion is to act like a narcissist yourself, and turn away from anyone flat and fake as an image on your computer screen—that is, from the twenty-first century itself. If we were all to do this, we would have an epidemic indeed. The script confirms itself, and the diagnosis and treatment confound the evidence, until it gets harder and harder to know whether people are really more selfish than ever before in the first place. In this way, it matters whether or not it's actually real, the epidemic, but it matters even more whether or not we *believe* it's real.

The question of the selfishness of others, though, leads quickly to the very difficult question of how we know things about others at all, and the mind-knotting question of how we know things at all. So I've cleared a good stretch of time, and interned myself in a little room at the side of the apartment I share with a boyfriend who is, suspiciously, like the millennial and the professional bad boyfriend, also from Atlanta, a trend that may require further examination. It's a strange, windowless room, more than twice as tall as it is wide, and for some reason there are electrical outlets near the ceiling, and a peephole in the door—it's like an apartment inside the apartment. It is not a good room, but I'm in here, in the kind of quiet you only get with a foot or two of snow, watching the world through that narrow peephole that is my computer screen, and reading as much of the Internet as I can bear, and whatever it refers me to, in order to try to get to the bottom of the question of the narcissism epidemic. In doing so, I hope to save you some time.

So enough about the setting, although it does bring up another version of the story, another villainous character to add to the murderer and the millennial and the bad boyfriend: the artist, or more specifically, the writer. A while ago I attended a panel on the topic of the presence of the writer's self, the *I*, in writing. On the panel were three esteemed writers, two female memoirists and a literary scholar, a man. As the panel progressed, the man began to speak about the narcissism of the *I* in literature. People often start out writing from their own experience, he said, in the first person singular. But then they grow up, and begin writing *he* and *she* rather than *me*, generously inventing on behalf of the *we*. The third person, he explained, is less selfish and more real than the first person: the reader can empathize more, if the writer gets out of the way.

It was a new twist on a story that condemned fiction in the first place, the story that spoke through Plato, who wanted poets kept out of his Republic because their fakery keeps us from knowing true being, and through Freud, who listed artists and writers alongside criminals in his description of those immature, vain characters who won't grow up and reckon with a disenchanted world, who suffuse the world with their own selves instead—a kind of character that Freud was one of the first psychologists to name as the narcissist. At any rate, I'm interested in the question of the epidemic because I want to know how to feel about everyone and the world and how to act, and because I'm worried about the future. But it won't surprise you to hear that I have a personal stake in the subject, too. I'm an essayist; I write the word *I* all day long, and I'm nervous when I do. More than anything, I don't want you to think me self-absorbed. So I will try to take up the topic of the narcissism epidemic objectively. If using the word *I* turns out to be a symptom of narcissism, you won't hear from me again.

Though there's a danger in this, too. The female memoirists on that panel may have had good reasons for writing about and from the *I*, but we didn't get to hear about them. When the writer was talking on about the generosity of the third-person, objective voice, its mature capacity to create empathy, they tried occasionally to speak, and the facilitator posed questions to them directly, to help. But the scholar just went on, saying not "I think this" but "this is true" and "this is how things are," and he did not stop speaking, and in the audience, it was harder and harder to breathe.

Diagnostic Criteria for
Narcissistic Personality Disorder

A pervasive pattern of grandiosity (in fantasy or behavior), need for admiration, and lack of empathy, beginning by early adulthood and present in a variety of contexts, as indicated by five (or more) of the following:

1. Has a grandiose sense of self-importance (e.g., exaggerates achievements and talents, expects to be recognized as superior without commensurate achievements).
2. Is preoccupied with fantasies of unlimited success, power, brilliance, beauty, or ideal love.
3. Believes that he or she is "special" and unique and can only be understood by, or should associate with, other special or high-status people (or institutions).
4. Requires excessive admiration.
5. Has a sense of entitlement (i.e., unreasonable expectations of especially favorable treatment or automatic compliance with his or her expectations).
6. Is interpersonally exploitative (i.e., takes advantage of others to achieve his or her own ends).
7. Lacks empathy: is unwilling to recognize or identify with the feelings and needs of others.

8. Is often envious of others or believes that others are envious of him or her.
9. Shows arrogant, haughty behaviors or attitudes.

Reprinted with permission from the *Diagnostic and Statistical Manual of Mental Disorders,* Fifth Edition (copyright 2013), American Psychiatric Association

The Epidemic

To have a disorder of the personality is, by definition—at least according to the bible of the profession, the *Diagnostic and Statistical Manual of Mental Disorders (DSM)*—to be an outsider in one's own life and a stranger to one's culture; in fact, in the *DSM*, "behavior that deviates markedly from the expectations of the individual's culture" is a crucial criterion for distinguishing personality disorders from anxiety, depression, and other mental afflictions. Those are things you *have*; they may come and go. A personality disorder is something you *are*. In the case of Narcissistic Personality Disorder (NPD), this means an entire adulthood of marked grandiosity and manipulativeness, vain idealization of self and others playing in endless rotation with injured withdrawal, coldness, and cruelty. Vanity and idealization are the narcissist's special qualities, but those diagnosed with NPD share a quality with other personality disorders, particularly those suffering from Borderline Personality Disorder, that makes relationships nearly impossible, and jobs difficult to hold for long: a self-esteem so fragile it is always under threat. To protect themselves, they do something called "splitting": they divide the world into good and bad and place the person or institution perceived to have caused the pain into the "bad" category, never to be trusted again. At best, this makes them incredibly difficult to be around. At worst, they are Anders Breivig, the murderer, who was diagnosed with NPD during his trial, and provides the case study that opens Anne Manne's *The Life of I: The New Culture of Narcissism*.

Since 1980, when NPD was first introduced as a diagnosis in the *DSM*, the American Psychiatric Association has claimed that less than 1 percent of the population suffers from it; in the most recent revision, the *DSM-5* puts the statistic, confusingly, at 0–5 percent, a range that reflects a good deal of variety, to say the least, in the methods and definitions by which psychologists define and measure this disorder. But many psychologists, journalists, and bloggers have, over the last ten years, argued that a personality disorder once used to describe those who could not fit in or deal with the rest of us is now, increasingly, the best label for most of us, that NPD is no longer markedly different from the expectations of our culture, but our culture exactly.

The popularity of the worst boyfriend ever, Tucker Max, might be evidence of this; he bragged about his narcissism (a diagnosis confirmed by a psychologist), and made millions doing so. Allison Mathis, the millennial who wanted to close down a busy Atlantan road, Peachtree Street, might be another. Allison is exhibit A in Jean Twenge and W. Keith Campbell's influential 2009 book *The Narcissism Epidemic*—they diagnose her, from afar, with "almost sociopathic narcissism," and return to her through-out as an emblem of millennial self-absorption, typical of a generation that Twenge named, in an earlier book, *Generation Me*.

In *The Narcissism Epidemic*, Twenge and Campbell report the results of the 2008 study that started it all. With collaborators Sara Konrath, Joshua D. Foster, and Brad Bushman, they conducted a meta-analysis of 16,475 surveys taken by American college students from 1979 to 2006 and showed that millennials are testing higher on the Narcissistic Personality Inventory than any generation before, at a rate greater than the increase in obesity. One in ten Americans in their twenties, they point out, has "experienced symptoms" of NPD, and one in sixteen of Americans in general. Such studies are reported in mainstream books such as *Narcissists Exposed*, *Why Is It Always About You?*, *The Object of My Affection Is in My Reflection*, *Disarming the Narcissist*, and *The Narcissist Next Door*, repeated in ritual cover stories such as Lori Gottlieb's "How the Cult of Self-Esteem Is Ruining Our Kids" (*The Atlantic*, July/August 2011) or Joel Stein's "The Me Me Me Generation" (*Time*, May 2013), and rehearsed on narc blogs and subreddits throughout the narcisphere.

It's easy to see how the traits of a personality disorder can spread through a culture like a disease. When you see someone else entirely concerned with his or her own hot-ness and not empathizing, you do it, too, like passengers on a plane who have to tilt their seats back because the person in front of them did. Soon, we all live "on that plane, with the disease of narcissism spreading like a virus through

the thin, recirculated air of modern American culture,"
write Twenge and Campbell, inviting us to join them in
the role of doctor: *The Narcissism Epidemic* is structured
like an epidemiology manual or an entry in the *DSM*, its
sections labeled "Diagnosis," "Root Causes," "Symptoms,"
and "Prognosis and Treatment."

Following these social psychologists' lead, bloggers,
journalists, and pundits have diagnosed not only the Kar-
dashians, Kanye West, and Donald Trump, but Dr. Phil
and Oprah Winfrey, Eckhart Tolle, Beyoncé, Jay Z, and all
men who have sex with women other than their wives while
holding political office—Anthony Weiner, Eliot Spitzer,
Mark Sanford, Kwame Kilpatrick, John Edwards, and Bill
Clinton, to name only a few. Narcissism is the favorite diagnosis for political leaders in whatever party opposes
one's own—either Paul Ryan is a narcissist, or Nancy Pelosi
is—and for policies: either the Affordable Care Act is narcissistic, or the privatization of Medicare is. Among the many
presidential narcissism memes in circulation is one that
superimposes over President Obama's face the *DSM*'s entire, lengthy definition of NPD. Celebrities and leaders have
often been accused of narcissism, of course, but when they're
named these days, they're treated as exemplary of what's
increasingly wrong with the world; the *Huffington Post*
blogger Ike Awgu finds Edward Snowden, for example, to
be exemplary of a narcissistic generation raised by social
media: "Twitter convinces them they are being followed
and are special and they imagine that they've 'connected'
to celebrities and others who they 'follow' or 'like'. The Internet has helped create a generation of deluded narcissists."

If narcissism has become more fluid and widespread, its symptoms distributed across the population, it has also become more variable, a fact tracked not only by psychologists but by bloggers and journalists who identify its various strains. If you are "reckless" and "self-assured" and a "social climber," you are a Phallic Narcissist. If you are in a group that thinks its members are more special than other people in the world, your group has Collective Narcissism. If you are the leader of a group, company, or country and are motivated by grandiose ego rather than care for your constituents, you are a Narcissistic Leader. If you are in a culture that prioritizes superficial symbols of power such as wealth and all you care about is competing for said symbols, then you are participating in Cultural Narcissism. If you are the leader of a corporation and you only have one thing on your mind—profit—then you are a Corporate Narcissist. If your company is so self-absorbed that, for reasons of high or low group self-esteem, it acts out of fantasies of grandiosity, ignoring reality, then your company has Organizational Narcissism. If you are a doctor who doesn't admit to fucking up a diagnosis, you are a Medical Narcissist. If on the surface you are really great in bed and seek out multiple sexual partners to confirm this, seeing in them not themselves but only the reflection of your greatness in bed, to compensate for your real, under-the-surface emptiness and inadequacy, rather than to actually care for and about said partners, and are unable to experience true intimacy, then you are a Sexual Narcissist. If on the surface you think you are really spiritual and seek out religious structures and practices to confirm this, seeing in them not a path to actually caring for and about others, but a story that confirms your spiritualness and connection to "the universe" or what have you, to compensate for your real emptiness and inadequacy, rather than humbling yourself in the face of divine and unconditional love and experiencing true religion, then you are a Spiritual Narcissist. If you are a scientist whose sense of your own genius leads you to dominate dinner table conversations and to think it's okay to have sex with the young boys you are studying, you are a White Coat Narcissist. If you are a normal, healthy person, but you become suddenly famous, or have upward of a thousand Facebook friends and also have children and/or a habit of going to upscale restaurants and photographing your food, you may contract Acquired Situational Narcissism. If you talk as if there are no other people in the room, even or especially if you are sneaky about it, such that the other people in the room don't even realize you are constantly steering the conversation toward yourself, even if it is to say something seemingly humble about yourself that is designed to get everyone to talk reassuringly about you for a while, or if you are just one of those people who go on and on and on and on and on and on, you are a Conversational Narcissist. And if you make an effort to act generously, publicly align yourself with important political causes and charitable organizations, talk a lot about care and empathy, and generally present yourself as exactly the opposite of whatever a narcissist is conventionally conceived as being, you are a Communal Narcissist.

Are all these diagnoses of emptiness measuring variations in the same kind of emptiness? How can the person who sucks the conversational air out of a room and the one who lights it up, the one who can't keep a job and the one who leads an organization, the one who is overly positive about herself and the one who is overly humble, the one who takes all and the one who gives all, have the same disorder? In the narcisphere, there are dozens of articles to help with these questions, with titles like "5 Early Warning Signs You're with a Narcissist" and "18 Signs You're Dealing with a Narcissist." These pieces recommend that on every first meeting we should be looking for symptoms, setting up tests to cut knife-like through potentially confusing smokescreens such as apparent kindness or intoxicating enthusiasm and joie de vivre or pure body-snatching sexual charisma. For example, "4 Narcissist Busters from the Minute You Say Hello" advises you to "Set boundaries," "Look for reciprocity," "Don't give it all away," and "Test if words get put into action."

If, despite these guides, you do end up loving someone who might be a narcissist, you may feel confused and alone. As Lisa A. Scott at www.lisaascott.com puts it, "No one knows what it's like to love a narcissist." Except people on the Internet; if you read on, you'll find www.narcissism uncovered.com, www.narcissismaddictionabuse.com, www .thenarcissisticlife.com,   www.narcissismsurvivor.com, www.narcissism-answers.com, www.narcissismcured.com, and www.narcissismfree.com, this last which promises to show you the "path back to self" when you've been "raped on a soul level." You'll find your own life described with uncanny accuracy by perfect strangers who seem to know you, and comments sections that are choruses of grateful recognition. "This article is 'spot on'! I was expecting to see a picture of my ex boyfriend at the end," is a response to "4 Warning Signs You're Dating a Narcissist," on PsychCentral. "I was considering taking him back, but after reading this . . . NO WAY!" Commenters compare horror stories about cheating husbands, about boyfriends and friends who have suddenly withdrawn— "something was not normal about how cold this person was"—and share advice about how to leave, how to cope with postnarcissist PTSD, and how to deal with the legal challenge of getting your ex-spouse's NPD confirmed by a professional so that you can keep him away from your children.

In the company of these websites, you can begin your "recovery journey." The websites lead you to books written by the same people who wrote the websites, books designed to deepen your understanding of the trap you've fallen into and how nearly impossible it is to get out without the support of a great deal of helpful materials from thenarcissisticpersonality.com, for example, which invites you to purchase the books *When Love Is a Lie* and *Stop Spinning, Start Breathing*. If it is your mother who has "ncism" or is the "narc" and you are a woman, you'll find www.daughtersofnarcissisticmothers.com, where Danu Morrigan wants to help you launch your recovery journey by helping you to understand why your mother cannot love you, what to do about it, and how to love yourself anyway, for which you will need the Mega Daughters of Narcissistic Mothers Resource Bundle, a $125 value that you can order on her website for $27. If you have hundreds of dollars and/or a particularly desperate case, you can get individual phone therapy with Danu Morrigan, who will teach you Emotional Freedom Technique.

Lisa A. Scott and Danu Morrigan and the rest will help you replace your own language for what until this point may have seemed a nebulous and hazy selfishness. Rather than just getting upset because your boyfriend is not talking to you as much as he used to, you'll recognize that he is "doing a discard"; it's common for narcissists to do this to their generous, empathetic, naïve girlfriends. The most important thing now is that you isolate yourself from the narcissist; you'll learn to call it going "no contact."

This is hard to do, so there's an app for it, called No Contact. When you are having trouble, you tap a button that says "Help! I need strength!" and the screen of your smartphone will encourage you:

Do NOT call them!
Move on, they're a lying manipulative @sshole.
Remember to block their calls and emails.
We must all let go of people who hurt us.
If they cared about you, they wouldn't have done it.
No Contact is one of the most hurtful narcissistic injuries you could inflict.
NC is your pure and sweet rejection.
Vent your frustrations in an online forum.

One such online forum is www.webofnarcissism.com. The site figures itself as a castle: in the Great Room, members share their stories; in the Library, they share research;

and so on. In the Garden Room, one can hang out alone and relax. In the rooms, the victims of narcissists learn to hone their "narcdar" for diagnosing "ncism" and their "narc"; call themselves "narcissistic supply"; help one another watch out for narc strategies such as "love bombing," "mirroring," "dosing," "silent treatment," "word salad," "triangulation," and "hoovering"; and find comfort when they experience a D & D (devalue and discard) or an IDD (idealize, devalue, discard). They learn there are two kinds of "no contact": NC (no contact), and NCEA (no contact ever again). They give one another advice on how to get phone numbers blocked and decipher the activities of their narcs, telling stories of terrifying, life-shattering husbands, unbelievably selfish mothers, lives broken by cruelties. It would be hard to find reading material more heartbreaking than these forum boards.

In some of the threads, though, you can see how the new language of the narcissism script could get you looking for narcissisms where they might not otherwise exist. "My narc in-law," wrote one poster, "removed the family pictures from the hallway, and replaced a living room chair with a piano. I just can't figure out why she would do this." In response, there are two or three thousand words of discussion from other narc victims on the matter of the piano. The narc in question claimed to put the piano there for the sake of an elderly father who loves to play. But this must be a smokescreen, since (a) the narc a priori can't be trusted; (b) the narc doesn't have genuine love or empathy, since she's a narc, so this gesture of "care" must be fake; and (c) said elderly father, according to the narc supply, doesn't even play piano very well, so what would motivate the narc to do this? What is she up to? From another poster: "My narc keeps all his Christmas cards in boxes. Why?" Maybe, speculates another narc feeder, trying to help, the boxes are a way of storing "supply," so that when the narc feels low, he can raise his self-image by looking at the cards. There's even a name, it turns out, for boxes in which narcissists keep greeting cards and other symbols of affection. One poster in the castle, who once wrote her narc mother, finds it particularly creepy that her narcissistic mother didn't talk to her about the letter but then kept it in her "trophy box" with other pieces of correspondence, Christmas cards, and notes of appreciation from coworkers and such. "She must take it out late at night," imagines the narc victim, "and feed on it."

Much of the script's language—no contact, narcissistic abuse, devalue and discard, cold empathy, narcissistic supply—was developed or popularized by Sam Vaknin, or this is what Vaknin claims. Vaknin is the author of the self-published *Malignant Self-Love*, which runs to 720 pages and is in its tenth edition. He claims to be a narcissist, a self-aware one, who makes his money explaining narcissistic men like himself to the mostly female audience for his books, who also populate his forum boards—he claims to moderate forum boards totaling twenty thousand members. But as the documentary *I, Psychopath* managed to catch on camera, when Vaknin was tested for narcissism, he scored rather low.

Sometimes those who are trying to help the victims turn one another. Vaknin is, according to a refugee from

his forum boards who runs www.maskofsanity.blogspot
.com, a psychopath masquerading as a narcissist in order
to cultivate a "cult following," someone who is "recreating
'Narcissism' and NPD in his own image, according to his
worldview"—in short, a fraud. The woman who writes
the Narcissistic Child website warns that the woman
who writes the daughtersofnarcissisticmothers.com
website should not be trusted—she goes by "Danu Morrigan" but is really Tracy Culleton, a "half-rate Irish novelist"
who also runs websites offering help for lack of confidence,
writer's block, and fear of clowns, all of which can be
helped by said "Emotional Freedom Technique," which is
best learned through expensive phone sessions with Tracy,
who is not a licensed therapist or a licensed anything. She
is a fraud, claims the woman who writes the Narcissistic
Child website. She is a vampire.

Vampire is a common word in the narcisphere, which
depicts narcissists as creating empty holes in the souls of
the people who provide their feed, thus duplicating narcissism everywhere they go, in a vampire apocalypse in which
people who are pretending to be people but who aren't,
really, who may even be trying to help you but aren't, really,
are walking around looking for real, normal, generous
humans upon which to feed—if you are an especially giving
person, warns the Internet, you are a prime target for
narcissists.

Like many apocalyptic tales, and like the NPD sufferer
himself, the narcissism story performs a splitting: the
weak and empathetic are victimized by the cold and dia-
bolical. It follows the pattern that the theologian Catherine

Keller contends shapes all our stories about the end of the world: "This pattern, always adjacent to suffering, rests upon an either/or morality: a proclivity to think and feel in polarities of 'good' versus 'evil'; to identify with the good and to purge the evil from oneself and one's world once and for all, demanding undivided unity before 'the enemy'; to feel that the good is getting victimized by the evil, which is diabolically overpowering . . ."

In the Narcissistic Parents room of the Web of Narcissism castle, there hangs a quote from Bram Stoker's *Dracula*: "They cannot die, but must go on age after age adding new victims and multiplying the evils of the world; for all that die from preying of the Un-Dead become themselves Un-Dead and prey on their kind. And so the circle goes on ever widening."

When members of the forum need a break from analyzing the actions of their real-life narcs and go to the castle's theater for recommendations of movies to watch and novels to read, they find movies and novels that are mostly about sociopaths and vampires. The castle imagery throughout the website is foggily gothic and melancholy in an Englandy way. The group members call themselves "keyboard faeries." Some members choose avatars depicting wispy Victorian-looking women or angels. If hanging out in virtual fog-swathed gothic castles or seeking entertainment in films about the very kinds of people they are trying to escape makes them look sometimes like they are fans rather than refugees in recovery, this is not really a topic of discussion on the forum boards.

"We are in apocalypse," writes Keller. "We are in it as

a script that we enact habitually when we find ourselves at an edge." The narcissism websites give you the language for a version of the script; the forum boards help you live inside of it, like living in a movie about the end of time. But this apocalypse can be a romance, just as romance is sometimes most compellingly staged when there is an impending catastrophe to be imagined.

The Bad Boyfriend

There is a moment when it is beginning to happen before you are conscious of it, and then it has happened and you try to remember when it was: it's as if he's turned a quarter circle to the left, away from you, from noon back to nine o'clock, dimming the light. There is nothing you can do, now, that will turn his whole face toward you. The eyes that gazed upon you with such life, lit up by you, are now the dark stone eyes of a fake, made thing or an animal, turning away from you. But you are real. Now you know it. *You* are real.

It's not something you would ever do to someone. Some people have called you a saint. You stick it out when things suck, are sweet when you want to scream. He, on the other hand, just does whatever he wants. It could be a "she" or a "he," but let's go with "he." You'd thought you were a "we" together, but all along he was an "I." You're crying and he is probably shining his little light elsewhere on some fool. It's as if he has some power over your life, over the lives of others, that means he'll never really get hurt.

Someone who loved you would care *more* when you cry *more*, but he doesn't understand crying. It's as if the more you cry, the more he swivels.

Maybe it is because he is so fragile that he cannot bear to be seen—intimacy issues, avoidant attachment style. So in love with you that he has to hide from you, in which case you should just be patient.

Maybe it's just a moment that anyone might have after being close to someone for months or years, the need to turn one's head slightly to the left, from noon back to nine o'clock, only to turn it back again with new and livelier eyes, in which case, maybe there's something wrong with you for freaking out.

Or maybe this is a thing that he has, that he is, the same thing that more and more men have, some essential, awful quality of twenty-first-century straight masculinity, and the end of romance: he's one of the evil fake.

You can debate these possibilities forever, but you're already in it: the story of the bad boyfriend, the narcisphere's favorite villain, the version of the script that is about the nightmare that happens *When* (as the title of one book on the matter puts it) *You Love a Man Who Loves Himself.*

"We may 'do an apocalypse' in our most intimate relations as well as in our most visionary politics," writes Keller.

Type in "he keeps withdrawing" or "what to do when he won't commit" or "how do I know if he's cheating on me" and you'll find Savannah at www.esteemology.com telling you about trauma bonds, about the way Stockholm Syndrome masquerades as love, because you've shared something—his cruelty—no one else can understand. She'll try to teach you to think differently, because she's trying to start a "self-esteem revolution" among women:

> The biggest mistake a lot of women make is they stick around way too long in their relationships . . . If someone is being disrespectful or they're blowing hot and cold with you—that means that they are not committed to the relationship—flat out.
>   . . . I often think of the song by Percy Sledge, "When a man loves a woman can't keep his mind on nothing else, Spends his very last dime tryin' to hold on to what he needs. He'd give up all his comfort, sleep out in the rain, If she said that's the way it ought to be."
>   —"Are You Involved with a Broken Down?: Understanding When It's Time to Fold Em"

You might think: that's it, exactly. He wouldn't spend his last dime on me. He wouldn't sleep in the rain. Where is the man who would sleep in the rain for me, and what's wrong with this one, who never would. I am addicted to someone who does not love me. I am unloved.

But there's a quieter, a worse thought: If I met a man that soggy and broke, would I even want him, after all? Because let's face it, there's something about the way this one turns away that's hot.

•

The narcisphere's chorus of advice about the bad boyfriend repeats and revises a story that is at least a hundred years old. Narcissism has always been, for psychology, a story about bad romance and desire gone awry, an account of how, when someone turns away, it means they're turning toward themselves, selfishly, and of what that means about what's wrong with the way you love, too. But in the beginning, narcissists weren't bad boyfriends, but women and gay men. The slide from the old characters to the new hints at something else the story is often about: what kinds of romance, and what kind of sex, should count as normal.

In 1897, Havelock Ellis, a British "sexologist," reported on the phenomenon of autoeroticism in a St. Louis journal called *The Alienist and the Neurologist*, using the term "narcissus-like" to describe people whose primary erotic object was themselves, who even during sex with others were turned on entirely by looking at and touching their own bodies, who masturbated way too much and seemed to prefer masturbation to fucking or being fucked by others. Ellis sent his journal article to a German psychiatrist, Paul Nacke, who published a piece on *Narcismus*, or self-love, in 1899 in the *Archiv fur Psychiatrie und Nervenkrankheiten*. Otto Rank also published a paper in 1911 on narcissism, in Austria, defining it more broadly than a sexual fetish, as "excessive self-admiration," and part of a homosexual orientation. For these early thinkers on narcissism, desire for those of the same sex was a perversion of real love, in which self-admiration was projected onto someone so similar he could serve as a mirror.

After seeing Nacke's piece, Freud wrote about the "narcissistic libido" in *Three Essays on Sexuality* in 1905, and took the subject up again in 1910, in *Leonardo da Vinci: A Memory of His Childhood*. And like Rank, he expanded the idea of a sexual fetish to describe a kind of personality. Based on a few scraps of evidence from Leonardo's writings and analysis of some of his paintings, Freud told a story of an absent father and a suffocating but overly beloved mother, a sexuality repressed—in order not to betray her—into an immature erotics, a desire for men who mirrored the self, sublimated into artistic and scientific genius. Freud admired—even, some would argue, identified with—Leonardo, and would do much during his career to argue for the treatment of homosexuality as part of a range of normal human attractions. But *Leonardo*, claims the historian Elizabeth Lunbeck, "sealed the deal": after the book was published, "narcissism and homosexuality were fatally entwined" in psychoanalytic orthodoxy. "Not all of the narcissistically inclined were homosexual, but it quickly became an analytic commonplace that all homosexuals were narcissistic."

A few years later, in "On Narcissism," Freud added to his portrait of queer self-adoration an analysis of "the type of female most frequently met with, which is probably the purest and truest one." Women, especially if they are beautiful, Freud wrote, "develop a certain self-contentment which compensates them for the social restrictions that are imposed upon them in their choice of object." This was 1914. He went on: "The importance of this type of woman for the erotic life of mankind is to be rated very high. Such women have the greatest fascination for men, not only for aesthetic reasons, since as a rule they are the most beautiful, but also because of a combination of interesting psychological factors."

To explain the psychological factors that made these cold, self-absorbed women so sexy, Freud compared them to children and animals: "The charm of a child," he wrote, "lies to a great extent in his narcissism, his self-contentment and inaccessibility, just as does the charm of certain animals which seem not to concern themselves about us, such as cats and the large birds of prey." Later, he added to this list primitive people, comedians, criminals, and artists: those beings who seem to have achieved a "blissful state of mind." It's a state of mind that normal, healthy people envy and desire, Freud explained, precisely because they've had to abandon it in order to grow up.

While he named it as a quality of femininity, Freud admits early on in "On Narcissism" that his theory was inspired by a broader problem: the way some patients—those paranoid and delusional people Freud called "paraphrenics," and some neurotics, too—turned away from treatment. Because of their "megalomania, and diversion of their interest from the external world—from people and things," such patients were "inaccessible to the influence of psychoanalysis." In other words, they weren't engaged in transference—the patient's repetition of past relations within the therapeutic situation, as Freud defined it elsewhere that same year. In addition to dreams and free association, transference is what provided the psychoanalyst's access to the patient's unconscious, his material for understanding how the patient lives and loves. As Freud would later describe it, in *An Outline of Psychoanalysis*, transference represented an inability to see the therapist as he was, as a "helper," an "advisor": "On the contrary, the patient sees in him the return, the reincarnation, of some important figure out of his childhood or past, and consequently transfers on to him feelings and reactions which undoubtedly applied to this prototype." The analyst's job was to notice this repetition, and bring it into consciousness. But this repetition involved at least one serious mistake on the part of the patient. Given the Oedipal romance that Freud thought scripted the path to maturity, in which the child mistakes his mother for a love object and his father for a rival, transference usually involved falling in love with the therapist, or projecting onto him feelings about a parent, or, in the case of women with a male analyst, both: a double mistake. But without these mistakes, analysis is thwarted, and the patient "cannot be cured."

Positing that pathologies like paraphrenia are states of arrested development, Freud worked backward from observing seriously delusional patients to describing resistant patients in general, and then developed a whole theory of early childhood development. Patients who do not engage in transference must be regressing, he reasoned, so the symptoms of their regression must tell us something about early childhood. From this premise, he deduced that all of us are born at the center of the world, uninterested in anything outside ourselves, not even able to distinguish between ourselves and others. When we grow up and learn to love, we forfeit a part of this early childhood narcissism—

impoverishing our oceanic, boundless self-absorption in order to care and be cared about. Genuinely loving parents teach their children it is safe to make this trade. But if a child turns outward from the natural megalomania of the toddler years to seek and give love and finds her parents cold, cruel, or violent, there is nothing to affirm her tender efforts. So she reverses course, veers inward, and attaches her searching affection to her own little ego, to be safe, retaining into adulthood the "omnipotence of thoughts" of early childhood. Narcissism is, in this sense, the sexual version of the instinct to self-preservation. And this initial portrait of narcissism hovers ambivalently between calling it a pathological trait and the most normal thing in the world.

That he characterized such immaturity as inherent to femininity, Freud wrote, was "not due to any tendentious desire on my part to depreciate women." It's just that while healthy straight men are capable of loving others outside themselves, gay men and the "type of female most frequently met with" tend to love narcissistically, treating others as mirrors of who they are, or were, or would like to be. Some women do develop along "masculine lines" and can love "in the masculine way," he admits; having a baby can offer a path out of narcissism for others, since "a part of their body confronts them like an extraneous object," leading them finally to care for someone other than themselves.

Perhaps the patients Freud called narcissists were people so lacking in empathy and capacity for love, so fraudulent and immature, that today they would be diagnosed with NPD. But one wonders whether any women and too-feminine men might have resisted making the mistakes transference demands—falling in love with the analyst, projecting their father-attachments onto him—for some other reason. From the perspective of Freud's emerging "science," if they didn't need therapy, their self-sufficiency must be a case of arrested development; if their sexuality was not visible as healthy from the perspective of the analyst's theories, they were immature. It's not something Freud considers, the possibility that such resistance might actually have been exactly what it looks like: an aversion to the analytic situation, with its imbalance of power, its detached and disinterested analyst, its required performances of colossal mistakes, its falseness and its theatrical repetition of the past, and that such resistance might make some sense, in a room where the patient's sexuality or gender is treated as something to overcome.

•

But why should these personalities most resistant to therapy be homologous with the types of people who are most attractive? "We are quite ready to accuse others of 'narcissism,'" writes the philosopher René Girard, "in particular those whom we desire, with the aim of reassuring ourselves and relating their indifference, not to the very minor interest that we hold in their eyes or even perhaps in absolute terms [. . .] but to a kind of weakness that afflicts others. When we do this, we credit them with an excessive and pathological concentration on themselves—with a kind of illness that makes them more sick than we are and consequently incapable of breaking out of their over-protected ego and meeting us half-way as they should."

In a 1979 critique of Freud's "On Narcissism," Girard suggests that what Freud diagnosed was not a kind of personality at all, not something some people are or have, but the ordinary dynamic of all desire. We're all performing self-sufficiency as best we can, Girard argues, though we've become selves by imitating others, in the first place; such dependence on others is our fundamental, existential state. We become friends and fall in love with people upon whom we can project our fantasies that there are some selves that are, unlike our own, replete unto themselves, and thereby irresistible. But it is we who've made a mask for them, and when they turn away, the mask inevitably falls, and we call them fake, as if they've tricked us. It's easier to diagnose them as narcissists than to admit to this, but there aren't any narcissists, according to Girard; it's only in relation to the fullness we fantasized they had that we then call them by the name of what our desire makes us feel: empty. Yet Freud was "really taken in," freezing the dialectics of desire into a powerful mythology about the immaturity and selfishness of especially attractive others.

There may have been personal reasons why Freud became so interested in the problem of the patient who turns away, and was so thoroughly taken in, layering onto the analytic situation the story of a bad romance. In *The Americanization of Narcissism*, Elizabeth Lunbeck explains that Freud wrote his book on Leonardo during the climax and dissolution of one of the most important relationships in his life, an intensely intimate friendship with Wilhelm Fliess, an ear, nose, and throat doctor who was, for some time, Freud's coke dealer. Beyond that, the exact nature of their intimacy is a matter of debate. The two exchanged hundreds of letters; Freud's friends thought Fliess a fraud and a charlatan. As Lunbeck shows, Freud's letters to Fliess are gravid with tantalizing metaphors; before one visit, for example, he wrote that he'd be coming with "two open ears and one temporal lobe lubricated for reception." Freud openly called Fliess the "love of his life" and reflected that his side of the friendship was feminine. Given the dearth of information Freud actually had about da Vinci, Lunbeck is not the only scholar to speculate that his biography masked aspirational autobiography, that da Vinci was a screen onto which Freud could project his own ambivalence about homosexuality, and perhaps his conflicted idealization of Fliess.

Freud's friendship with Fliess ended disastrously (Fliess accused Freud of stealing and disseminating some of his ideas about bisexuality without permission), leaving Freud—by his own account—wrestling to overcome his homosexual desires. He still had to revise the Leonardo book. While he did, Freud traveled with another close friend, the psychoanalyst Sándor Ferenczi, to Sicily, a trip that both seemed to have highly anticipated. Despite having sent dozens of passionate letters to Ferenczi in anticipation of the trip, however, once they arrived in Italy, Freud reversed course, treating Ferenczi as his secretary, suddenly more interested in working on the book alone than in spending time with his companion. When Ferenczi objected,

Freud performed what the narcisphere calls "doing a discard": he left him, Ferenczi complained, "out in the cold" for the rest of the trip. For his part, Freud criticized Ferenczi for idealizing him, for imagining him omnipotent, something that, Lunbeck argues, Freud had done to Fliess. In her account of these relationships, drawn from letters between the men, she speculates that Freud was cruel and cold to Ferenczi in order to get over Fliess and, in that way, accomplish his goal of transcending his homosexuality—that is, his femininity and dependence. But his longing for Fliess would persist for years, just as Ferenczi would reportedly remain wounded until his deathbed by Freud's devaluing of him. No wonder, then, if in the wake of all that homoerotic heartbreak—everyone wanting the one who didn't want him—the analysis room became a hall of mirrors, where analysis and even early childhood would be understood in terms of thwarted romance, and spurned and vulnerable friends or lovers could try out powerful diagnoses, to numb the pain.

If "On Narcissism" helped Freud to shift his concerns about his own femininity onto female patients and gay men, the stakes of this mistake were high. It sutured female and gay sexuality, devalued self-sufficient femininity as a kind of selfish trickery, and idealized a normal male sexuality that overpowered both femininity and homosexuality via passage through the Oedipus complex, ideas that would repeat throughout twentieth-century psychology until they landed, stripped of this lineage, in the narcisphere. There, the story would turn from identifying the self-absorption of women to condemning the vanity and immaturity of straight men, and then slide and turn again— this story about how some people are, which under the surface is also a story about the way that we all want.

•

Four years after "On Narcissism," Freud wrote "The Uncanny," in which he attempts to explain those objects and humanoids and experiences that give us the shivers: "that class of the terrifying which leads back to something long known to us, once very familiar." Here, Freud approached again the magnetism of beings on the edge of the human, of mannequins, puppets, clowns. When we encounter the creepy, he speculated, there is a flash of remembering all we have overcome to become adult, that time when we felt all as one, spoke to our toys, believed the magic we made with our minds. Or a flash of remembering what we have surpassed, culturally, to become civilized—that Freud shivers at the number sixty-two, seen too many days in a row, means he is believing, for a moment, what primitive people used to believe: that there is some meaning and intent in the universe, that there might be some reason why he, when walking in a provincial Italian city (this is another example he gives) keeps getting lost and ends up, again and again, in the red-light district.

While much of the essay is taken up with a long reading of Hoffman's "Sandman" story and a belabored explanation of all uncanny phenomena by means of the Oedipal threat of castration, in this essay the centrality of that complex seems forced, and so Freud keeps circling round, and repeating himself, unsatisfied with his central theory's explanatory power. Perhaps because it embodies the form of the essay, what stands out is Freud's returning, again and again, to the red-light district accidentally, and not even commenting on this, telling us something without telling us.

Freud never really says it, but fear is not our only response to the uncanny. We fear ghosts, zombies, clowns, puppets, vampires, and narcissists, and yet we are drawn to them. And what are those prostitutes in the red-light district to him, to which he returns again and again, if not living women who will act as things, as dolls, and dolls who will act like women. He doesn't talk about narcissism in "The Uncanny," but if we were to put the two essays in conversation, Freud might have to agree with Girard that the narcissist's magic comes, at least in part, from us.

•

So there you are trying to decipher the blank space left when your boyfriend turned away, researching and diagnosing. Savannah is trying to train you to stop wanting uncannily attractive bad men. What she tells you—what everyone tells you—is that when someone blows hot and cold, you have to get better at knowing when to fold 'em, and when to run. But the banner image above "Are You Involved with a Broken Down?" and just under the scrolling "Top News" ("I See Dead People, I Mean Narcissists"; "Are You Mistaking Intensity for Intimacy?"; "Are Narcissists Aware of Their Behavior?"; "Why Do I Still Love

Him?: Understanding Trauma Bonds") features a black-and-white photo of a good-looking man on a motorcycle. He's turning his head away, but while he does, he's opening his leather jacket and slipping it off his shoulders to reveal his six-pack, in some kind of narcissist striptease.

You can keep researching until you figure out how to kill your attraction through diagnosis, you can study and agonize and try to treat all you want—he'll probably never figure out what you're up to. Even if he goes looking, there are no "Are you in love with someone who's martyring out?" websites—websites that explain how at first she idealized you, telling herself you were the best man she'd ever met, and kind of glossing over in her head the more negative qualities you so charmingly explained—your great love of beer, your tendency to brag when insecure, your need to watch Ultimate Fighting Championship ten hours a week, the way closeness sometimes freaks you out—but who now takes these things as personal affronts. There are no websites that explain how, because of what she has been reading, you are beginning to present as a fake, entirely self-absorbed person lacking in empathy, who cannot be helped, and from whom she should run.

If you do catch her researching, or sitting around quietly watching you, lip trembling, and ask her what's wrong, she'll say, "Nothing!" and smile widely, changing in an instant. It can be spooky, how unrelated what she says is to what seems to be going on inside. You have no fucking idea how much time she spends hunched over the computer reading PsychCentral, or sitting on the couch staring at the wall, thinking about the difference between who she thought you were and who you are, and attempting to diagnose. So it might start to seem as if what is inside her is an emptiness, into which all your good intentions and most concerted attempts at taking out the trash and quitting drinking and also just kind of being yourself just slide in and dissipate. As if there is nothing you could do to fill her up, no action, no matter how generous, that could change her story.

If, on the other hand, you type in "my girlfriend's gone mad what do I do," or if it is you, as a man, who finds himself on the other end of the dynamic, consistently rejected by women, and you type in "my girlfriend is suddenly cold" or "how do I get a woman to love me or at least fuck me," you won't find the narcisphere. You'll find the manosphere, that portion of the Internet that's developed over the last decade since Neil Strauss's *The Game* sold 2.5 million copies, a decade during which Tucker Max sold 3 million copies of books full of tales of rating and berating women, using and losing them. You'll find the "seduction community," and blogs like "The Rational Male," "Inimitable Men," "Return of the Kings," and "Alpha Game," which will urge you to take the red pill, realize you've been emasculated by feminism, aspire to being an alpha male, and mock betas. From the Red Pill subreddit's hundred thousand–plus subscribers, you'll read examples of the victimization of men by women, learn that rape claims are often false, and hear mantras like "Believe you're better than everyone else" and "Take women off their pedestals," and "Their rejection can't hurt you." Here, you can join a renaissance of masculinity where seduction strategies meet palaeo diets, confident men embrace conflict, dominance is your evolutionary right, and certain passages of *Fight Club* are repeated like scripture.

It is not a secret on the manosphere that this is all about acting more like a narcissist; you're practically berated into it. Seduction-game strategists, like the blogger James C. Weidman (a.k.a. Roissy) at Chateau Heartiste, will teach you to intentionally attempt to replicate the traits of narcissists and sociopaths precisely because these traits are hot. The gurus advise a courtship that alternates between charming and insulting, fucking and disappearing, staging the rhythms of the bad-boyfriend script in order to trap women in obsession and "dread." You do all this because, as Weidman will tell you, "A man who is full of himself is full of a woman's love." What you're learning is a pragmatic and—given the victimization and emasculation of men by the manosphere's sworn enemy, a role played by Jezebel.com—a *necessary* narcissism: if you want women, you've got to start dominating them right away, because this is what women secretly like. Tucker Max, at least, has the data to prove it: half of his readers, his Facebook likes, and his Twitter followers are women.

So the next time you do see your girlfriend on the couch with her laptop, looking at you curiously, lower lip trembling but then pasting on that fraudulent smile, you'll know what she's doing: she's trying to dominate you. It might be time to get the upper hand.

"It would be wrong to believe," Girard writes, "that the deceivers at this game are sharply separated from the deceived, that the world is neatly divided between the cold calculators and the innocent dupes. Everybody is a little of both; you must be a dupe of your own comedy to play it with conviction. The romantic and satanic vision of the cold calculator, of the totally lucid manipulator of other people's desires, is a more sophisticated version of the narcissistic illusion."

As psychoanalysts debated and deepened Freud's understanding of extraordinary self-absorption, some would accept his oppositions between deceiver and deceived, between self-regard and the capacity to love, and fill in the lines of his portrait of the narcissist until it became the image we have now: a charming mask covering a cold calculator, a self empty of empathy and the capacity to love. But others emphasized the role of self-love in narcissism, which Freud had, after all, called a normal part of human development; they argued that self-admiration and care for others were reciprocal and mutually enhancing. The debates over narcissism were part of a larger argument about how we know and help other people at all. Ferenczi himself emphasized the crucial role of empathy in the face of a resistant patient, and was excommunicated from Freud's circle; Donald Winnicott, in England, created an alternate theory of early childhood development that emphasized the mutual mirroring between mother and child, describing narcissism as a rich source of healthy ego and love. The story of these arguments, and of how the focus of psychology shifted from neuroses to personality disorders such as narcissism in the middle of the last century, has been told many times, most fully in Lunbeck's *The Americanization of Narcissism*. But it's worth pausing briefly with one of those debates—between Otto Kernberg and Heinz Kohut, whose disagreement turned on the question that haunts any girlfriend of a bad boyfriend: how much can you, and should you, empathize with someone who might be a narcissist, and when should you draw the line and fight? This was a disagreement that hinged on different approaches to what should happen in the therapy room, but also how to see the world.

Both Kernberg and Kohut were Jewish psychoanalysts who fled Austria in the 1930s—Kernberg to Chile, and Kohut to England—and later arrived in the United States, where they established influential practices and schools of thought. Psychoanalysis had focused on hysterics and neurotics, whose failures to negotiate between the demands of work and society and their own instincts left them nervous and ashamed, but Kohut and Kernberg became interested in patients complaining of emptiness and meaninglessness, and concerned with the failure of orthodox psychoanalysis to understand the disorder Freud called narcissism.

The problems Kohut saw in his midcentury American patients were meaninglessness and isolation; with these patients, he began to abandon Freud's detached, objective analytic method, and practiced unconditional care for the patient and empathy. Only by putting himself in the patient's shoes, Kohut argued—through "empathic immersion"—could the therapist really understand a patient who matched Freud's definition of narcissism. And from that perspective, the disorder, if it was a disorder, looked quite a bit different. He illustrated this in the case study of "Mr. Z," whom he analyzed first from a classical perspective, and then from his emerging "self psychology" method of "vicarious introspection." Analyzed through the lens of the classic Freudian method, the story of Mr. Z is familiar: an excessively attentive mother; an absent father who returned to threaten his love of his mother; a retreat to the easy gratifications of infantile self-absorption and grandiosity, which, when challenged in therapy, manifested in rage. But Kohut noticed that Mr. Z's self-sufficiency was a mask, and that when confronted, he expressed a deeply pained and insecure self. In psychoanalysis, Mr. Z learned to be more realistic, and Mr. Z left therapy able to work and maintain relationships, but returned several years later complaining of a lack of joy, of sexual satisfaction, of any sense of meaning in his life. This is when Kohut tried empathizing with him, rather than viewing him as a man stuck in childhood. Taking Mr. Z's perspective, Kohut began to see that he was not rebelliously trying to retreat to an infantile state, but trying to leave it. In turn, he came to view early childhood narcissism as relational, rather than individual, and as a generative source of self, love, and creativity, provided it was mirrored and accepted. It is when their exuberant fantasies aren't mirrored in the world, Kohut argued, that those accused of narcissism retreat; they're capable of empathy, and empathy can allow them to continue to draw on the resources of ambitious self-regard, even as adults, rather than protecting themselves behind a mask of shallow self-sufficiency. His treatment of narcissists informed his emerging therapeutic method, "self psychology"; what he'd seen working with those called "narcissists" led him to reject Freud's theory of drives. He argued that the self wants to be whole, and to love; this wholeness is a force that pulls patients toward healing. Selves know, he thought, what they need to grow; some are just trying to learn the steps toward love a little late. By generously empathizing with the narcissist, Kohut argued, the therapist can begin to cultivate a kind of fellow feeling, and the patient can grow up.

Kohut was optimistic; his empathetic method and belief in the unceasing movement of selves toward wholeness and love were tied to a hopeful worldview, at odds with Freud's dark vision. While Freud had written about the analyst's ability to walk in the shoes of the patient, Kohut's emphasis on empathy was deeper, and heretical in the way it shifted power in the consulting room. Late in his life, he wrote, "If there's one thing I've learned during my life as an analyst, it is the lesson that what my patients tell me is likely to be true—that many times when I believed that I was right and my patients were wrong, it turned out, though often only after a prolonged search, that my rightness was superficial whereas their rightness was profound."

Kernberg was not so hopeful. Hewing closer to Freud's sense of the self as a battle between violent and unacknowledged desires and drives, Kernberg focused on the narcissist's aggression, and recommended conflict and confrontation over empathy. He, too, acknowledged the healthiness of early narcissism, but when it persisted into adulthood, he argued, it must be treated as a pathological self-regard. The diagnosis reflected his belief about how "psychodynamic" therapy should work, developed in his classic and difficult book *Borderline Conditions and Pathological Narcissism*: rather than providing unconditional empathy for the patient's position and self-views, the therapist's job was to challenge the narcissist's efforts to control and to doubt his grandiosity at every turn. The empathetic therapist colluded with the narcissist's delusions; Kohut's method could only hurt the narcissist further, Kernberg argued, and fuel his rage. As Kohut and Kernberg sparred throughout the 1970s, it was Kernberg's version of the narcissist that would attract the attention of the press and lead to the creation of the Narcissistic Personality Inventory in 1979 and the inclusion of NPD in the *DSM* in 1980. The methods and writing style of psychoanalysis—Kohut and Kernberg's nuanced immersion in the details of a patient's life over time, and the careful teasing out of complexities in language—disappeared behind a list of traits, five out of nine, a way of knowing if someone has narcissism, or doesn't, and the belief that if they do, they are among the hardest patients to treat. In addition, Kernberg's more orthodox Freudian view had won: narcissism was understood as a condition of a failed self, difficult to treat, not a source of well-being and love, not a dynamic between people.

On the question of prevalence, this first *DSM* entry was cagey: "This disorder appears to be more common recently than in the past, but this may be due only to more professional interest in it." But behind that neat list of narcissistic traits, within psychology's ever-expanding and dividing fields and schools, the debates continued: How much self-regard is normal, and how much unhealthy or even evil? When someone is acting like a six-year-old, should you empathize with their view of reality or try to correct it? If someone doesn't want to talk to you or fall in love with you, when is that because he is fundamentally an asshole? If someone turns suddenly away from treatment, or from a relationship, does that mean she is incapable of love? Are there really people who have no empathy? Can you help someone learn to love? And is this thing called narcissism something some people are, or something they do? These are questions you can ask forever, not only if you are a psychologist, but if you find yourself loving someone who turns away.

After Kohut's death, incidentally, his biographer Charles Strozier would discover that his case study of Mr. Z was actually a memoir, a study of himself—that in order to argue for the triumph of his psychological method over those of Kernberg and Freud, he had narrated the disastrous analysis of his own narcissism that he had undergone with Ruth Eisler, and then described the empathetic analysis he wished he'd had. Placing Kohut's case study in a long and venerable history of psychological case studies faked from autobiography—a history that goes back to Freud himself—Strozier cautions, "It is a slippery slope from science to solipsism."

•

One of the episodes on Tucker Max's blog is titled "Tucker Has Moment of Reflection, Ends Poorly." A girl comes over to his place, just before her date with another guy, to give him a blow job. Afterward, he's gloating about how badass he is, and then he starts thinking about the guy, and he realizes: "OH SHIT! HOW MANY GIRLS HAVE DONE THIS TO ME?" He goes out to some bars to research this possibility, getting wasted in the process. When he confronts a friend about it, the friend points out that Tucker has done this very same thing, been with more than one person in a day, many times. This shocks Tucker, and this friend, Tucker tells us, is no longer a friend. "Like I wasn't already mind-fucked enough tonight." He drinks more, surveys girls to see if they've been with more than one man on the same day, until he's so drunk he is, as he describes it, shouting things like "I'm famous, girls can't do this to me."

And then he locks eyes with someone gorgeous: "Piercing blue eyes and sandy blonde hair. Great body. A deep, penetrating stare that belied a wisdom and understanding beyond the average person. Great charisma. And we had immediate chemistry." He dances with this person for an hour, flirting, and "every smile was met with a smile, every caress with an equal caress." It's him, of course, he's dancing with his reflection in the dark back room of a Chicago bar, and it's a rendition of the urtext of the narcissism script, Ovid's story of Narcissus, though at the end of this one, Narcissus doesn't turn into a flower, but passes out in a park. Upon waking, Tucker stumbles home to look in a mirror again:

> The "love of my life" stared back at me with a face covered in hardened, crusted vomit. Yellow and brown bile matted my hair . . . (the author will spare you further description, here) . . . So much for

being too good for whores' sloppy seconds. But the pièce de résistance lay on the top of my head, stuck to the crusted vomit . . . a small, dry, hardened dog turd.

If Max seems to be playing the role of the bad boyfriend on purpose by gesturing so explicitly toward the myth he's fulfilling and then offering himself up for bawdy punishment, this is only the most obvious example from his oeuvre. That only an asshole would want to perform narcissism is not, of course, lost on Tucker; that's the point, at least on the surface. But it's hard to believe that Max's readers would miss his deeper point, here, about empathy— that the inability to put oneself in the other's shoes makes for a crisis, when you encounter the selfishness of others, and paradoxically means that you'll end up only finding yourself in the world (and, incidentally, that self-absorbed straight alpha masculinity is a mirror away from looking rather gay).

Max's insight gels with Girard's theory that our inability to get out of our own shoes when we encounter the selfishness of others can mean that what we end up diagnosing in them is our own fear and desire. When diagnosing and understanding others is your very livelihood, this might mean that the narcissist looks different depending on what is visible from the perspective of your method and what you fear. If the narcissist became, over the course of the last century, a particularly good screen on which to project our biggest questions about selves and others, the answers were as different as the psychologists answering them. If the method is the talking cure, in which the patient must fall in love, and you're trying to overcome your own femininity, she begins as a woman resistant to psychoanalysis, a figure of a kind of femininity that must be overcome, so different from your method's favorite characters (for a long time, neurotics) as to seem a stranger, and for this reason unsusceptible to the "influence of psychoanalysis." For the psychologist who emphasizes empathy, she is the patient lacking in empathy, and only empathy can heal her. For the psychologist whose method is confrontation with reality, the narcissist becomes the patient who this method cannot reach and is nearly incurable. For clinical psychologists, the narcissist became a category, five out of nine traits, maladaptive and malignant, and nearly untreatable. And now, when psychologists must publish popular books, and it is women who consume self-help books about relationships, the narcissist changes from a woman or a gay man into, more often than not, a particular portrait of a macho, self-involved, immature, and unreliable straight man, and it is women who are more commonly victims, and who the narcisphere's self-help addresses and advises if you *Love a Man Who Loves Himself.* The gender of the archetypal narcissist shifts according to who's got the power of diagnosis, and if there's one thing a girl with a bad boyfriend has, it's the moral upper hand in the religion of mental health.

•

Despite the way he seems to be winking at his readers in the blow job/mirror/dog shit sequence above, Tucker might resist our calling his narcissism a performance, or at least he did in 2009, when explaining to Cinemag why he didn't care what his mother thought of his assholery: "My mom, no question, is not happy with it. The narcissist act is not an act. I actually am a narcissist, very much so. My world revolves around me. She's my mom, I care, but not really."

But in 2012, he began recanting the narcissism that had fueled the soggy, sportfucking twenties that had made him millions, and helped to inspire a generation of men to join "seduction culture," although Tucker, it should be made clear, hated all those other guys, the PUA guys. His narcissism came, he argued then, from a deep self-loathing that prevented him from feeling empathy. When he decided to clean up and go to therapy, he chose classic psychoanalysis, four days a week, and began announcing it in national magazines. The story he told Michael Ellsberg at *Time* magazine, for example, was a Freudian one. The days of benders and blow jobs were "all id." "What I'm trying to do right now," Max said, "is connect my ego and my superego to my id. I'm trying to understand, why was I doing all this stuff?" He's rewriting the story of his promiscuity: the sex was trauma sex, the girls had daddy issues. He wanted a woman who's a real "partner" now. With the girls who tried to befriend or sleep with him, he was an evangelist for psychoanalysis. He got his girlfriend, Veronica Pike, into it; she's learning to "feel her feelings" together with Max.

Now, three years later, they've married and had a baby, and he's paired with an evolutionary psychologist to publish a dating book, *Mate*, that encourages men to be the best they can be—"no seduction techniques," "no bullshit," just an "ethical," "honest" dating manual for the post-fratire man. The book cover reverses the logic of the cover of *I Hope They Serve Beer in Hell*: Max's hot wife, Pike, is pictured next to Max, whose face is blanked out, and over the blank is printed "Your face here."

Neil Strauss, the author of *The Game*, is reforming, too, and his own therapy has led him to write a book called *The Truth* that teaches men to seek real, mutual relationships with women. Understanding where it all came from—the game, the seduction community he helped to form, all that pragmatic narcissism—has been, he told Kathy Gilsinan at the *Atlantic* in 2015, "the biggest shock of my life":

> Strauss: Well, myself who wrote *The Game*, Robert Greene who wrote *The Art of Seduction*, and Tucker Max who, well, is Tucker Max—what do we all have in common?
>
> Gilsinan: What?
>
> Strauss: We all have narcissistic mothers.

At his pickup artist workshops, Strauss went on, he used to ask men in the audience how many of them had overbearing mothers who only cared about themselves. About eighty percent would raise their hands, every time. And if more straight men start reading (as Max and Strauss hope) self-help books on how to have healthy relationships, the prototypical narcissist will change genders again. It's a script that can be performed again and again, because its oppositions are so intuitive, so stable—there are villains and heroes, narcs and victims, the abnormal, selfish them and the healthy, empathetic us—that the gender and sexuality of the characters that play the roles can keep changing, in order to distinguish, at any particular moment in history, what is right and good (i.e., mistaking your therapist for your dad/lover, renouncing your desire for people of the same sex, procreating, having meaningful straight sex in a monogamous committed relationship) from what is not (i.e., masturbating too much, avoiding therapy, giving a blow job to someone on your way to a date with someone else, and also getting a blow job from someone on his or her way to a date with someone else). The characters change, depending on who's wielding the power of diagnosis, but the movie stays the same.

The Millennial

We know this one cold: on her episode of *My Super Sweet 16*, Allison says exactly what we would expect. "I get what I want," she says, and "I love to shop." At Justin's, P. Diddy's club on Peachtree, she recites, "So I've been thinking about my grand entrance, and I think we should shut down this block. Completely. And have a parade." There's a cut to a party planner looking behind him at Peachtree Street, raising his eyebrows in disbelief, and a brief sound clip of a marching band. "That's gonna be almost impossible . . . on a Saturday, at seven?" "They'll have to detour"—she trips on the word, as if she's trying to say something she's been coached to say, or something's been cut, and repeats "detour, because my sweet sixteen is more important than wherever they have to be." "Nobody ever closes Peachtree," the planner says. "And you know there's a hospital right here. What if there's an emergency, an ambulance needs to get to the hospital?" "They can wait one second," she says, "Or just go around!"

This is the story of the self-absorbed millennial, indifferent to the sick and dying, indifferent to us. Allison turned sixteen on television in 2007; according to *The Narcissism Epidemic*, her "almost sociopathic narcissism" is typical of the generation now poised to rule the world—"Generation Me." Allison begins their book because she looks like the future, and now the romance—for people tend to adore the younger generation for their beauty at least as much as they deplore their self-absorption—turns into an end-times tale.

It isn't the first moment in history that has been called exceptional in its selfishness, or the first time a new generation has been called narcissistic. For every article on the millennial narcissism epidemic, there's one pointing out that as long ago as 1976, Tom Wolfe's "The Me Decade" announced from the cover of *Time* that some disturbing irrevocable thing had happened to the culture, a self-centered falseness of frightening proportions, and that three years later, in 1979, the year before the *DSM* first included NPD as a diagnosis, Christopher Lasch's *The Culture of Narcissism* hit the bestseller lists. There's something called a "generational fallacy" and, it's tempting to say, dismissing the young as narcissists is just its newest incarnation.

But the prophets of the current epidemic acknowledge that there have been exclamations about worse-than-ever self-centeredness before; this does not discourage them from their thesis. If there's an epidemic of contagious and toxic self-absorption, it makes sense that it would have started at some point, and grown over time. In fact, they locate the narcissism epidemic's beginning in precisely that decade, when the communal and social justice impulses of the 1960s turned into individualism and obsession with celebrity culture, and est and orange jumpsuits, which are two examples Twenge and Campbell give, reached peak popularity. During the 1970s, "Even music and entertainment switched from communal experiences like Woodstock to disco and cocaine—both activities done in groups, but while dancing or getting high on your own (except for the Hustle)." Here, the authors seem to oppose even the drug use of the 1960s—the community-oriented highs of marijuana and acid—to the selfishness of cocaine use. Like Wolfe and Lasch, they collect some entertainingly random anecdotes in support of their thesis. But unlike Wolfe and Lasch, when they talk of an epidemic, they have the data to prove it, thanks to a new quantitative methodology— cross-temporal meta-analysis—that tracks psychic states and personality traits over large groups of people over time. It is this method that leads them to claim that since Lasch first identified the new narcissism, things have gotten worse.

These new claims of an epidemic come from a field— social psychology—that is after something that's hard to get to in the hall of mirrors of the therapy room: replicable knowledge about how culture influences individuals, how psychic states are shared among groups and change over time, how one's attitudes toward others influence one's actions. Quantitative social psychologists, like Twenge, seek an objectivity that would solve the problem of having as many narcissisms as psychologists who study them;

they standardize measures of personality, and crunch massive amounts of data to get beyond the local scale. Their methods are designed precisely to show us when we're doing things like making the generational fallacy; they're poised to help us escape the inevitable narcissism of our historical position.

This relation between the larger culture and the individual is what Lasch was after, too: "Every society reproduces its culture," he wrote, "its norms, its underlying assumptions, its modes of organizing experience—in the individual, in the form of personality." In the late seventies, he argued, that "form of personality" was a version of Kernberg's narcissism:

> Notwithstanding his occasional illusions of omnipotence, the narcissist depends on others to validate his self-esteem. He cannot live without an admiring audience. His apparent freedom from family ties and institutional constraints does not free him to stand alone or to glory in his individuality. On the contrary, it contributes to his insecurity, which he can overcome only by seeing his "grandiose self" reflected in the attentions of others, or by attaching himself to those who radiate celebrity, power, and charisma. For the narcissist, the world is a mirror . . .

For Lasch, as for Kernberg, the narcissist's self-regard masked emptiness, and his self-sufficiency, vulnerable dependence. Lasch, however, thought this version of narcissism was endemic in 1979 in part because of the self-esteem movement, with its ideology of personal growth. Self-help and consumerism, he argued, offered shallow solace for such "impoverishments" of capitalism as shitty jobs and the bureaucratization of every aspect of life. In this he differed from Wolfe, who had blamed the new narcissism on prosperity, though their jeremiads blurred in the popular mind. And he seemed to miss the fact that one of his sources, Kohut, was arguing that self-love was not narcissism, but its cure. There would be a deeper, historical irony, too; arguably, it's Lasch's translation of Kernberg's narcissist that echoes loudest through the narcisphere, showing up on websites such as Esteemology.com, in the service of the same self-esteem movement he skewered. But his point wasn't to show that individual boyfriends and mothers and young people should be vilified, but how therapy, bad work, wealth inequality, and consumer culture influence the individual psyche.

If this point resonates less than his portrait of the creepy, empty, false self, it may be because of the way he argued it. Once Lasch had borrowed from Kernberg his theory of the vain, fake, dependent narcissist, he worked by a kind of deductive reasoning, accumulating examples that become uncannily similar once the premise is assumed, a way of knowing—apocalyptic reasoning, we might call it—common enough in books (not to mention to any individual having a particularly bad day, or year). In his apocalyptic catalogue he indexed not only the rise in therapy and self-help, and radical feminism, but confessional writing, memoir, metafiction, shallow humor, ironic detachment, middle managers, the designated hitter rule, the sexual revolution, and permissive parenting. Even an increase in astroturf in professional sports stadiums suggested to Lasch that fakery was on the rise. Into this catalogue of late-twentieth-century narcissisms, he dropped quotes from psychologists and other cultural commentators and nostalgic reminiscences about religion, the "Protestant work ethic," and patriarchy; Lasch spent a chapter in lament about radical feminism and changing gender roles. In this way, he tried to show that things were really getting worse than ever before, and that "narcissism" was the name for this worseness. But when it came to NPD, in 1979, this kind of claim was not yet, as the old joke about Freud goes, "testicle."

If the claim is now testable, it is thanks to an innovation dating from that same time, when NPD was added to the *DSM* and *The Culture of Narcissism* hit the bestseller lists. In 1979, two social psychologists, Robert Raskin and Calvin Hall, developed a survey that measured traits of NPD in "normal" and "healthy" people: the Narcissistic Personality Inventory. The survey presents you with forty pairs of statements that are equally socially acceptable—"I am assertive" and "I'm not very assertive," for example—and whether or not you would agree with either, you must choose one (it's a kind of measure called, appropriately, a "forced-choice" survey). The pairings ferret out maladaptive facets of narcissism, such as vanity (A. I don't particularly like to show off my body. B. I like to show off my body). There are also claims such as "I like to take responsibility for my decisions," which, if you agree with it, pushes your score in the narcissistic direction, but is not necessarily an antisocial trait. Social psychologists like Raskin and Hall assume that there is no one point on the spectrum at which one becomes a full-blown narcissist, and in fact, in the paper that presented the inventory, they emphasized that even a score of forty on the test would not qualify one as having NPD. The survey is supposed to be able to measure "subclinical" narcissism, even though the traits it measures are based on the definition of narcissism as a personality disorder. But in the reporting of NPI results in the popular press, the pathology and the normal blur into one word.

What can such an inventory show about us? Of course, you might choose different statements on different days, or at different points in your life, or depending on how much you understood about what was being measured. But in the three decades since the invention of the NPI, the measure has been widely tested for validity, demonstrating that high NPI scores correlate positively with attention-seeking behaviors, aggressive responses to threats, taking more than giving, lack of empathy, and valuing fame and image over family and community. It is a measure that, some thirty-five years after its invention, has made it possible to claim that millennials are more narcissistic, that narcissism is contagious, and that as a result, the future looks like NPD.

We have been talking about measures and methods all along—how the means we use to understand others influence our understanding—and we're going to have to keep talking about it now. Reader, if during the last chapter's attempt to summarize psychology's debates over narcissism your eyes glazed over, it's only fair to warn you that things are about to get worse. But it is not only Allison's status as an "almost sociopathic narcissist" and a whole generation's selfishness and therefore the very future that is at stake, here. It is you, if you've ever taken an SAT or an IQ test, the Meyers-Briggs or some other personality test to determine whether you deserve an education, a job, a promotion, or a good OKCupid match. It's probably not too much of a stretch to say that the social psychology measures and methods that produce the claims of an epidemic—surveys, psychometrics, demography, meta-analysis—are in charge, in very real ways, of your future.

Since 1979, many psychologists have administered the NPI to college students. Twenge's innovation was to collect 16,475 of those surveys, calculate the NPI scores, average the scores across all available campuses for each year, and then track these scores for the years since the survey began. What she and her collaborators found was, indeed, that NPI scores had risen between 1979 and 2006. It's an increase that is widely reported as "30 percent," though what that means is, as we'll see, a matter of debate. To support this cross-temporal study, Twenge and Campbell cite other cross-generational studies, by other social psychologists, that support their hypothesis. Some describe a generation markedly more inflated in their sense of self than previous ones. Millennial expectations for education and career are higher (in 2010, 60 percent expected a professional or graduate degree, for example, compared to 30 percent in 1976), but their results remain the same; only

9 percent obtain degrees. More millennials expect well-paying jobs and promotions than actually get them. Millennials also score higher than previous generations on surveys measuring extrinsic, rather than intrinsic, values. And they score lower in empathy, which has declined in college students since 1979, even as their belief that the world is just (which implies a lack of compassion for the less fortunate) has risen.

But when Twenge and her collaborators compared narcissism scores to self-esteem scores, they discovered that both rose together. This raised the problem of what they were finding. Was it really narcissism, given that narcissism had long been considered a cover for low self-esteem? Rather than doubting that what they were measuring was narcissism, Twenge decided that one hundred years of qualitative research had been wrong: rather than a cover for a shattered, insecure, and empty self, narcissism must be exactly what it looks like—overly high self-esteem. Her narcissists were not empty, like Lasch's and Kernberg's, but too full of themselves. Their problem is that they actually think they are better, feel more special, and genuinely believe they are more important than everyone else. What really causes narcissism, then, must not be cruel, cold parenting, but too much parental love, attention, praise, friendship, and permissiveness: everything, Twenge and Campbell argue, that Baby Boomers lavished on millennials. And things are getting exponentially worse; parental coddling is replicated across the lives of young people, now, by social media, and by reality television microcelebrities like Allison, who Twenge and

Campbell call a "superspreader" of the disease of positive self-esteem.

Perhaps there is a thing, narcissism, that has changed this much over time: from a self-sufficient femininity, to a hollow, crushingly low self-image, to an empty and dependent low self-image masked by fake high self-esteem, to too much real self-esteem. Or perhaps we're talking about different things entirely. Yet when Twenge, Campbell, and other prophets of the epidemic in the field of social psychology talk about Allison and the whole millennial generation, they draw on the power of the older version, our fears of the uncanny mask over an empty, vulnerable self, when the narcissism they're measuring looks, on the ground, like something else entirely.

These results have been widely rehearsed in the mainstream press. When Twenge and Campbell's initial 2008 paper on the epidemic first came out, it was immediately covered by major news networks, such as Fox and NPR, and a hundred newspapers, and it has been referenced in journalistic pieces and echoed throughout the narcisphere in the years since. This coverage seldom spends much time on the considerable disagreement in the field of social psychology over what the NPI actually measures, and whether the math actually represents a significant increase at all. It's easy to miss that when psychologists claim that "By 2006, two-thirds of college students scored above the [NPI] scale's original sample average, a 30 percent increase in only two decades," what they mean is not that pathological narcissism has increased by 30 percent, but that a slight majority of students in 2006 answered, on average, one or two more questions in the narcissistic direction than did those in 1986, when the sample average was first determined—and that this is not an increase considered significant by other researchers. It's easy to forget that the NPI measures "normal" and "healthy" narcissism. It is less frequently reported that other research has demonstrated that the rise in scores has been in subscales that are "adaptive," rather than "maladaptive," traits. It is rarely reported what Twenge has, in debates behind the paywalls, herself admitted: the only significant increase in NPI scores over the last three decades has been among female college students. This, other psychologists argue, might be a good thing, if agreeing with statements such as "I like to take responsibility for my own decisions" represents an increase in agency among women.

Working with the same data set Twenge and Campbell used and adding a few more campuses, another group of psychologists, led by Kali H. Trzesniewski, determined that scores on the NPI were not rising in any substantial way. Using data from the Monitoring the Future Project, which has surveyed American high school seniors since 1976, other psychologists have demonstrated that self-esteem levels have not risen at all.

How could researchers find such different results? One problem is that all data gathered regarding narcissism are self-reported. Yet in disclaimer sections that are common enough in psychology papers on narcissism to constitute a kind of ritual, social psychologists always admit something like this: "narcissists are necessarily bad at reflecting on their own experience." In terms of the narcissism/self-esteem connection, Erin Myers and Virgil Zeigler-Hill attempted to track the direction of that bad reflection, using fake lie detector tests. They found that women, at least, who test high on the NPI tend to report high levels of self-esteem when they think they can get away with it—in other words, that reporting high self-esteem is part of the mask narcissists attempt to maintain, despite their crushing insecurity—but lower levels of self-esteem when they believe that others might be able to discover that they are lying about how they really feel. With other collaborators, Zeigler-Hill found that different facets of narcissism correlate with differing levels of empathy, emotional intelligence, and the ability to have a theory of mind—that is, to understand the perspectives of others; surprisingly, people who scored high on "grandiosity" are more empathetic.

For all of these objections, Twenge has answers. The debates devolve into squabbles over sample sizes and the validity of measures; terms are defined and redefined, and assumptions shift. The cause is an important one: to find empirical evidence for our connection to our culture, and the way social and economic structures influence us. It is this kind of work that enabled Émile Durkheim, a century ago, to show that suicide, that most individual of actions, is itself a social object, influenced by religious belief and other historical variables. Such debates are part of the work of social science, and of any science, but in the narcissism debate, when social science tries to get a grasp on the psychic states of the individual via answers to surveys, the acrimony is especially acute.

One cause may be the heavy pressure on academic psychologists to publish positive results. A 2010 metastudy of papers in psychology found that 80 percent achieve positive results; the odds of a psychology paper confirming its hypothesis are 50 percent higher than a paper in the hard sciences. Studies that report null results are less desirable, though extremely helpful to other researchers in terms of getting to the truth. Such publication bias means, according to some critics, that meta-analyses like Twenge and Campbell's, which draw their results only from studies that are published, in the first place, are particularly vulnerable to inaccuracy—that in this case, inaccuracy is multiplied exponentially. And in a 2015 metastudy of quantitative and experimental psychology papers, 270 scientists attempted to replicate a hundred studies in cognitive and social psychology published in top journals in 2008 and found, dismally, that only 38 percent of results were replicable.

The most recent revision of the *DSM* took ten years. Arguing that the facets of narcissism are so complicated or "dimensional" that narcissism may not be a discrete category at all, some members of the APA tried to remove NPD from the new edition. They lobbied to replace it with a more flexible diagnostic method, which would identify patterns of behavior rather than categorizing distinct personality types. The APA decided first to remove the diagnosis of NPD, and then, after considering alternate versions, to put it back in, the criteria slightly reordered but virtually unchanged from the *DSM-IV*. They added the trait-diagnosis method in an appendix, so that now, the user's manual of the profession is frozen in ambivalence about whether the term even describes a useful category at all.

"There is still more work to do," concluded the authors of the verification study, "to verify whether we know what we think we know." Such caution is reflected throughout the work of social science and in Twenge and Campbell's long, painstaking research, too (if less so in their public proclamations and in the reports of their research in the popular press). Behind the paywalls, the questions continue. Are people who test as narcissists more successful in late capitalism, or less? Is narcissism correlated with high self-esteem or crushing emptiness/low self-esteem? Is self-esteem correlated with success? Are rising narcissism scores in the general population correlated with economic prosperity or downturns? Is it right to treat narcissism as a "disease," albeit a disease spread via culture and tipping-point effects? Is it even a thing at all? But in the narcisphere, the epidemic research is incorporated, ignoring not only the controversy but the new findings about high self-esteem, and narcissism is still usually portrayed as an emptiness, a hollow shell covering crushingly low self-esteem, all the same.

The contradiction—the narcissist is nothing he seems, and everything he seems—reflects a change from therapeutic to quantitative methods. Despite or because of its efforts to achieve objectivity and its valiant and necessary efforts to try to capture what's happening to us and our personalities on large scales, even quantitative social psychology must define its narcissisms relative to the way in which they are viewed. The narcissism of interest is a collection of variable traits—manipulativeness, self-admiration, vanity, fraudulence, grandiosity—which is exactly what can be measured across large groups of people, if they are willing to answer survey questions. The narcissism of interest is social and contagious, because what is being measured is what can be seen across a large sample, a certain generation, what is shared: no one individual who takes the survey will have NPD, but gather enough individuals together, and the group will. The narcissist of interest confirms the central assumption of psychometrics—we are who we are in relation to others, to groups, to culture—and the villain in this version of the movie is the one who denies that relation, is unempathetic, indifferent to her connection to her society, at the same time as she exemplifies it: she's too full of herself, just as she appears to be.

Or she is exactly the opposite. The social psychologist Jeffrey Jensen Arnett, who has been one of the foremost critics of the Generation Me theory, has argued that the current crop of young people is in actuality the most conscious of their relation to others, the most generous, the most empathetic, of any generation we have seen. One of Arnett's arguments with Twenge was staged in the journal *Emerging Adulthood* in 2013. He debunked her taxometric methodology, her "convenience samples" of college students, and her interpretation of her results; lined up numerous studies disproving her conclusion; and then listed stats that show that millennials are more other-centered and responsible: car accidents and crime have declined, volunteerism is up, teen pregnancy is down, and millennials are the least racist, sexist, and homophobic of any generation in history. "Given all the favorable trends in young people's attitudes and behavior over the past 20 years," argues Arnett, "whatever we have been doing in our socialization of children, we should keep doing it."

If Arnett is right, the story of the millennial narcissism epidemic returns to myth, where it began, in Ovid's pool in the forest. To call it myth, though, is not to dismiss it. Any monsters that feel so real must speak to us somehow. And so, in the tradition of Lasch and many popular social science trade books, the narcissism books tell stories. In *The Narcissism Epidemic*, we meet Camille, a San Diego girl who claimed that "feeling special is a great form of motivation"; Lauren, an Atlantan girl who wrote in a *New York Times* comments section that self-confidence is important for success, and "if that's the definition of a narcissist, [I'm] proud to be one"; a governor who put money in the state budget for classical music CDs to be distributed to the parents of newborn babies so the babies would be smarter; a preschool that has a TV studio, so that toddlers can make their own television shows; another preschool, where three-year-olds are led to sing "I am special / I am special / Look at me"; Linda, who laments the big narcissistic houses all around her, telling the authors that in contrast her parents "raised six children in a 1,200-square-foot, three-bedroom house with only one bathroom"; a person who in one month used 400,000 gallons of water, and this during a citywide water ban; and, in the beginning and repeatedly throughout *The Narcissism Epidemic*, Allison, who wants to close down Peachtree Street when there's a hospital across the street.

•

On the Amazon site where you can download episodes of *My Super Sweet 16*, there is only one consumer reviewer, who gives the show only one star. "It's a dumb show," the reviewer explains, "but it is useful in teaching my kids about how some children are plain out disrespectful and spoiled." MTV assumed people were hate-watching; they followed up the series with a spin-off called *Exiled*, in which the beleaguered parents of the sweet sixteeners could send their children off to try to make their way under harsh conditions in remote villages in the third world, and followed that with a scripted show, *My Super Psycho Sweet 16*.

In her episode, when she says the ambulances can just go around, even Allison seems to be laughing at the ridiculousness of what she's saying. "Oh my," says the party planner, theatrically. "If Allison wants it," says Allison's mother, robotically, "make it happen." On party day, Peachtree does appear to be closed down; one suspects MTV had a hand in that. There is a parade, with a marching band, horses, and motorcycles, and Allison arriving in a limo, exclaiming, "I win! I'm the coolest person ever." Midway through the party, there is the requisite drama—a sick friend throws up on her and she kicks him out ("It's

the worst thing that's happened to me in, like, four years!").
Then G-Unit takes the stage and everyone starts dancing,
her parents give her the keys to a Mercedes SUV, and everyone agrees that it's the best party they've ever been to, as
they do at the end of every episode, cut to commercial.

In Stanley Milgram's famous early social psychology
experiment, people proved that they will do terrible things
in unreal situations when compelled by a convincing authority. Milgram asked hundreds of men to administer
shocks to someone they believed to be also a subject in the
experiment, though this other person was really an actor.
The subjects believed they were participating in a study
on memory; they'd say a word to the other man, and if he
failed to repeat it correctly, they were instructed to turn a
dial that administered a shock. The lowest shock was
labeled 15 volts, "slight shock," and the highest, 450 volts,
or "Danger: severe shock." As the participants increased
the imaginary voltage, the actor would emulate pain and
plead to be let go. Some of the men backed out early, but as
many as 65 percent, in one version of the experiment, kept
going until the highest imaginary shock was administered,
and the actor fell silent.

Milgram published his study in the *Journal of Abnormal and Social Psychology* in 1963, and reflected on its
meaning in *Obedience to Authority* in 1974. "The social
psychology of this century reveals a major lesson," Milgram wrote in the book. "It is not so much the kind of
person a man is, as the kind of situation in which he finds
himself that determines how he will act." It was not some
essential personality trait that motivated participants to

keep hurting others, Milgram argued, not sadism or something like that, but a shifting of responsibility onto someone else or an institution, what Milgram called an "agentic state": *I'm just a part of something, a cog in the wheel of something important.* "The disappearance of a sense of responsibility is the most far-reaching consequence of submission to authority," he wrote.

And yet a social psychology experiment, Milgram himself wrote in 1976, "smacks of dramaturgy or theatre. The experimenter carefully constructs a scenario to focus on certain aspects of behavior, a scenario in which the end is unknown and completed by the experimental subject." In her essay "Revisioning Obedience," Kathryn Millard reveals how Milgram's experiments were scripted, costumed, rehearsed, and filmed for dramatic effect: the simple story that he presented, made available to postwar audiences with the Eichmann trials fresh in their minds, was that the overwhelming majority of us would do atrocious acts, compelled in the right way. If administering shocks troubled the participant, if he asked whether he should go on, the experimenter would say "Please continue," and then "The experiment requires that you continue," and, if questioned again, "It is absolutely essential that you continue," and then, if they still resisted, "You have no other choice; you must go on." The way this piece of theater went, Millard argues, Milgram met with nothing but obedience—his show was painstakingly controlled to replicate the kind of power dynamic that would lead citizens to support genocide—yet the experiment's own power structure and stagecraft forcibly limited its results.

Milgram employed a level of deception that the discipline deemed unethical, so researchers haven't been able to replicate his results until recently, when a virtual reality experiment, and one done on television with lower-level fake shocks, found similar percentages. But in the years since, psychologists and other researchers have looked for what he might have missed, what other details of the experiments and the participants might have mattered. Millard's essay is included in a 2014 special issue of *The Journal of Social Issues* that catalogued some of these revisions; papers argued for the important role of participants' beliefs, and emphasized what Milgram's papers and film, *Obedience*, obscured: how much, and how often, they disobeyed.

It has been from the beginning the work of social psychology to discover the circumstances that matter, when it comes to understanding how people act. The therapist has time to do the long, slow work of learning the details, forming an understanding of the client, getting a perspective on the life that she has lived. This is harder to do at the speed of lab experiments or surveys, which can tell us much about trends across large groups, but do not have much time for the details of individual lives. We need all these different ways of knowing. But when the stories of real people are told at lightning speed in support of studies reported as objective despite being deeply contested, it's worth asking what we really see. It's worth asking, too, how much we can tell from a performance on television—which, in the case of reality television, might seem to replicate a similar power structure as Milgram's experiment, in order to get subjects to perform like narcissists, exactly as we would expect.

It's a power structure that is inherent, too, in the act of making an argument about real people in writing.

Allison, with her "almost sociopathic narcissism," is pressed into the service of an argument, like Lasch's, that proceeds anecdote by pop culture anecdote—a story told not in the manner of the slow, detailed, meandering, essayistic work of Freud and the psychoanalysts, but at great speed, in a state of emergency. At this speed, the new narcissism myth emerges: it's not that Allison seems normal but does evil things. It's that because she looks evil, she must be evil; her sin is being exactly as she seems on television.

If the psychoanalytic researchers of narcissism distrusted the narcissist's surface, finding beneath the mask of her self-sufficiency an emptiness, the social scientists who prophesy an epidemic trust that surface entirely. They must take what their subjects present at face value, rely on what they report on surveys or perform on television, because, lacking time and contact, that's what they can see. It's our problem, too, for the Internet is an anecdote machine, and the new narcissists, glimpsed online and on surveys and on TV, must be both full of themselves and as thin as paper or a computer screen, just as they appear. Yet Allison appears this way only in a theatrical situation that likely put some pressure on her to perform, and then in the theater of a book that begins with and returns repeatedly to those few moments on TV, and then, once again, in the book you are reading now, which, to make its point, itself ends up making shallow portraits of people and ideas and social psychology studies that are, in every case, much more deep.

•

It takes only a brief Internet search, though, to flesh out a bit more about Allison's life. She was raised in a prominent African American family in Atlanta's wealthiest neighborhood, Buckhead. Her father is the late Charles A. Mathis, Jr., lawyer to TLC, Usher, and also the Southern Christian Leadership Conference. He was a brilliant litigator—an artist in the courtroom, reportedly—and renowned for throwing some of Atlanta's best parties. "Everyone knew," a friend was quoted as saying in one of his obituaries, "how Charles got down."

Allison has grown up to marry DeQuan Jones, a basketball player. They run a foundation together, JetJones, that helps impoverished children in Atlanta succeed in school. She does family genealogy. These days, she writes a lifestyle blog, livelifewellblog.com, that encourages women to look good, be educated, and travel. You can shop her wardrobe, and read her thoughts about marriage, family, basketball, and travel. In a list of the twenty-five favorite moments in her life so far, she reports that the moment she loved, on the day of her party, was one "before the cameras started running," when she and her mother shared breakfast in bed and talked, as they often did. She answers every commenter on her blog kindly. She comes across, in other words, as a real sweetheart. Allison also reports on her blog, incidentally, that she has just run her first 5K, and she's proud of it, but she didn't love doing it. Her first 5K will be her last.

Allison also grew up wealthy in a city whose wealth inequality is, according to a recent Brookings Institution report, the highest in the nation, ahead of San Francisco, Boston, and New York, and more than twice the national average: in Atlanta, the 5 percent of households at the top have twenty times the money as the whole 20 percent of households at the bottom. Another study, in 2013, demonstrated that Atlanta's poor have a harder time moving into a higher class than those in any other metropolitan region. And Allison grew up black in a country where white families have 90 percent more wealth than African American families, on average, even when controlling for education levels—a gap that hasn't changed in twenty-five years.

Which of these details might matter when it comes to understanding why Allison celebrated an extravagant birthday party, on television? We do not yet know; we shouldn't even pretend to. But if she is a representative of a generation, it's one that faces considerable economic hardships. This cold winter, in the United States, less than 50 percent of citizens have full-time employment. If you are unemployed, your chances of getting a job are one in five for the first five months, one in ten if you've been unemployed six months or more. If you're looking at a minimum-wage job, you'll need two or three of them. If you have a minimum-wage job, there's a good chance you've been to college—half of minimum-wage earners have—and college debt averages $30,000 per graduate.

It is easier to talk about the inappropriately grandiose

dreams of the young—to go to college, to get promotions—as narcissistic than to talk about the various reasons why these average dreams will be thwarted. Lasch was vehement in describing the way that an increasingly unfair economic system called upon its subjects to perform shallow self-esteem. But the current prophets of the epidemic, while they lament the rise of easy credit and the economic hardships facing the average family, report the narcissism of their subjects with moral outrage, and invite readers to take a position outside that culture, as diagnosers and wary victims. In this apocalyptic moral drama, Allison plays her part, though we in the audience are less likely to be duped into thinking that Allison, the real person, would do those things at all if she weren't compelled to compete on our behalf, and to perform as the pathologically selfish rich girl we can condemn, so that we might remain the empathetic ones, the good ones.

·

In her classic book *The Drama of the Gifted Child*, the psychologist Alice Miller gently hypothesized that one of the most likely careers for people heavily invested in projecting a false self is psychology itself. Themselves often children of cold and selfish parents, therapists develop, from a young age, "special sensitivity to the unconscious signals manifesting the needs of others," and a strong motivation to employ this skill to manipulate people, under the mask of empathy. "Who else," writes Miller, "without this previous history, would muster sufficient interest to spend the whole day trying to discover what is happening in the other person's unconscious?" The book is widely considered to be about narcissism, although Miller manages, blessedly, never to use the word.

The Drama of the Gifted Child was first published, in German, in 1979. Since then, at least one psychometric study has tested Miller's idea that narcissists tend to turn up most often in the profession of psychology, correlating NPI scores with career paths, and found that Miller is wrong; more often, people with high NPI scores end up in business. But when psychology is conducted by surveying college students, by "convenience sample," the data are gathered most often from the college students in psychology classrooms. This—not just college freshmen, but college freshmen enrolled in psychology classes—is not only the cohort from which Twenge and Campbell's thirty-year study was mainly drawn, but (according to one metastudy) the one upon which 67 percent of psychology studies are based—which makes one wonder how much of the understanding of the self, of mental health, of "normal" and "abnormal" psychology that we gather from announcements of new studies in our Twitter feeds, would actually be more accurately framed as an understanding of what young psychology students think about themselves.

If it seems a rather selective sample, this is a matter of considerable discussion and concern among psychologists themselves. But it may not be such an inaccurate sample if we consider how much the discipline permeates our lives, not only through therapy but by means of the methods that educators use to evaluate and place us, managers use to manage us, and corporations use to tabulate our every virtual move in order to find correlations that will provide marketers whose methods were developed by this very same field with the secrets to selling us what we then believe we need. To cope with the pressure, we study the Internet's translations of therapeutic psychology, and are taught to think positive thoughts, remember to be grateful, and do an altruistic act every day so that we'll feel better. It is a private labor made increasingly public and compulsory—corporate gurus advise CEOs to hire Chief Happiness Officers and score their employees on their levels of well-being, firing the saddest 10 percent, and even our governments have been encouraged by the United Nations to instate Happiness Indexes in order to measure how well we're doing at this, how hard we're working at positive thinking. To relax, we take Buzzfeed personality quizzes, as if to scratch some enjoyment out of the very kinds of measurements that determine our success, and even at the bar, we sit down and talk of our progress toward mental health—"I think I really figured it out. I think I'm getting better"—and diagnose our family members and lovers and friends.

Or you don't do all these things; one hopes to God you don't. If the prophets weren't sure we're using "I" too much, your writer would say, more accurately, "This is how I am, sometimes," or "Sadly, this is what I do."

But if you do at least some of these things, maybe college students studying psychology *are* a sample that represents us after all. Maybe it's no wonder that prophecies of an epidemic of self-regard should feel so true, and that we should fetishize a warm, natural empathy, at the same time as we click and click to get the next hit of objectivity, the next PsychCentral post about the three things we can do to most efficiently increase our happiness or the five ways to know our boyfriend is cheating—as if there were someone outside the lab who could see better than we can what to do and how to be.

And every reality television show offers a chance to watch what others do under such observation, how narcissistic they look under the pressure to compete, assert, value themselves, in situations only a little more surveyed and surreal than our own. For a moment, we get to pretend we're outside the lab, watching Tucker and Allison perform what we're often called upon to do but are supposed to deplore in others. While we watch, we get to pretend we are psychologists, for a moment, but while we do it we're laughing. We're cracking up.

After her episode of *My Super Sweet 16* aired, Allison didn't get sent to a remote, third-world village to suffer for her narcissism; she went to the University of Miami to get a B.A. in psychology.

The Murderer

Still, there is the murderer. In prison, he is no longer smiling. This is a relief; it is especially when he smiles that he travels across the edge of what we can bear to include as human, because that's when he looks most like someone we might like to know. It's uncanny: what is monstrous, strange, inhuman, looks, for a moment, too much like what is familiar, normal, human. Or vice versa—the familiar and warm looks, for a moment, too much like what is strange and cold.

·

We know this already; *uncanny* is our everyday word for a surprising resemblance.

·

He complains of his conditions: his PlayStation does not have the games he likes, his room lacks a view, and all he wants to do is write apocalyptic memoirs and manifestos about how women and Muslims are growing in power and must be overcome but the rubber pen he's been given cramps his hand. In a twenty-seven-page letter to the government of Norway, this man who has murdered seventy-seven people describes said pen as "an almost indescribable manifestation of sadism."

•

It is against coldness, our story about the narcissism epidemic, and wants connection. It wants empathy, this movie about how the murderer's disorder is contagious, about the cold calculators among the next generation, next door, in your house, in your bed. It expresses a great longing for kindness. The sensation of understanding among people is the story's great, forsaken good. A lift in mood: Maybe the story's popularity, these days, implies an epidemic exactly opposite to the one it describes. Maybe it shows an increase in how much we now cherish kindness; we deplore and fear narcissists because empathy is, increasingly, our highest value.

But the moment you begin to find that the other lacks empathy—when you find him inhuman—is a moment when you can't feel empathy, either.

•

On a subway platform, the writer is searching through her bag because she's had an idea so important it must be remembered and delivered to the world. Her hand comes out of her bag covered in ink: the pen has broken, everything is ruined. In a tiny and insignificant moment of the day, beyond which in this instant she cannot see, she rages

for a moment at the cruelty of the world and all its shitty
pens.

•

"We are in apocalypse," like a script we act out, again
and again. The script, Keller writes, is neither good nor
bad. Sometimes it helps us leave awful relationships, flee
genocide, start revolutions; sometimes, though, it's a "civilizational habit." We get addicted, imagine the evil that is
growing in power is outside us, and then the movie we're
in enables our "numb complicity" in the disasters that are
happening. When what you do is scripted, it is meaningful,
but you're not really responsible. Sometimes, on the other
hand, being in apocalypse leads us to some righteous violence we think is heroic. The murderer is "in apocalypse,"
in this sense, but when we imagine he is not like us, or
that everyone else is increasingly like him, we are in it, too.

•

Kohut and Kernberg fled genocide to give us an endlessly
contradictory account of the encounter with human evil—
how, they asked, could anyone go so cold?—that would be
taken up and transformed, despite their great care, into a
story that divides us, by defining empathy as something
we have and others lack.

But in order to do this, the narcissism script defines
empathy quite narrowly. It gives us a moral scale that begins at human empathy, hits "unrelatable" somewhere in
the middle, and ends at an evil that can only be described
in terms that oppose it to the human: machine, beast. It

tries to separate the genuine and empathetic from the not empathetic and fake in a moment when we're more aware than ever that those categories don't hold, if they ever did.

Milgram's documentary *Obedience* screened at the same time as everyone was following the Eichmann trials, trying to understand: How could so many humans act so much like beasts?

A year after his experiment, researchers at Northwestern University found that, unlike your average human, rhesus monkeys would starve themselves rather than pull a chain that administers an electric shock to a companion.

•

"You may not like what I am going to say," begins an essay by the philosopher Adam Morton, called "Empathy for the Devil." What he is going to say is that when we are struggling to understand the actions of someone who has done something wrong, it is seeing ourselves as humane, as "morally sensitive" or "decent," that most limits the accuracy of our empathy.

Morton defines empathy the way we commonly think of it, as sharing feeling with another. But being a philosopher, he is quite careful in how he defines this sharing: "One person, A, has empathy for another, B, with respect to a particular state of mind, when B experiences an emotion or attitude and A has a representation of B's state which shares its affective tone and perspective." Empathy is not just a shared feeling, for Morton, but an accurate sharing of an emotion or belief that captures not just the content but the tone of it, and an experience of the place, the perspective, from which the other's emotions and actions come. The word Morton uses for this sharing is *representation*. To get this accurate kind of sharing, the kind of empathy that would matter, is much harder, Morton argues, than we tend to think. It is especially so when we encounter acts of violence, and everyday acts that seem so self-centered they slide easily into the category of evil.

When we try to understand others, Morton says, we inevitably do so from our own position, by comparison to ourselves. This point of view limits us to identifying "a small number of relevant factors, holding others implicit." We focus on those factors we recognize superficially and quickly from our own lives, but because we are so invested in viewing ourselves as "good," we often miss the most important ones. We do this constantly; we have to in order to live, but this is one of the reasons, Morton writes, that Milgram's results shock us. And yet it is important that we do a better job of it, particularly when it comes to the devils among us.

•

To illustrate this, Morton tells a story: a man gets angry at a co-worker who's working too slowly, shouts "If you wanted to take so long, you should have started early at work instead of taking time to get pretty for your fag friends," and then begins pummeling him. The attacker is arrested, incarcerated, and a volunteer counselor is sent to visit him. The volunteer is a decent man, not someone who would ever beat someone up, and he wants to help.

Assuming that the inmate must be, unlike him, homophobic, he looks for a way to empathize. He remembers a time he got angry at a cab driver, in a racist way, shocking himself. Compassionately, believing himself decent and that it is therefore decency, too, that the inmate has betrayed, he remembers this breach in fellow-feeling, imagines this incident as existing on the same continuum as the inmate's violence, and confesses it. By sharing this experience of stereotyping and anger with the inmate, he thinks he is able to help him, and feels better about his volunteer counseling.

But what if the counselor's empathy by analogy from his own experience, Morton asks, is totally off-base? And here he gives us a theory of action that goes like this: We don't generally, as Kant imagined, measure a bunch of options carefully and then reason our way to pick the most generalizable, ethical one. We don't have time. Or even if we do, each option may have pros and cons, things that are benefits and things that are barriers to carrying it out, and who is to say what really pushes us to choose? But every time, something pushes us toward crossing one of those barriers rather than the others. If we can identify which barrier mattered, which thing the person overcame in order to act, Morton proposes, we might really get a sense for the affective tone and the person's perspective. Usually, when we're thinking about the violence of others, and we consider ourselves decent, we tend to think the barrier they've overcome is morality itself. But what if that is not really the barrier that mattered? To try this out, Morton must tell more stories, stories that *might* be analogous to the violence that sent the inmate to prison.

An addict, a woman who has quit smoking, is comforting a depressed friend who wants to smoke, so under the guise of comforting her friend, the first woman buys a pack, smokes a cigarette with her friend, and starts smoking again.

A shy man, long in love with a woman he barely knows, runs after her to give her a book she has left behind on a bus seat. Amped up on adrenaline from the run, despite himself, he finally finds the guts to ask her out.

A queasy woman, disgusted by dog shit, can't bear to pick up her dog's shit with a plastic bag. But she mistakes a bit for a piece of chocolate cake, and scoops it up easily, and from then on, she discovers that if she pretends dog shit is cake, she can do it.

In these stories, the most important barriers overcome on the way to action are, Morton explains, resolution, timidity, and disgust. And here is what he asks us to imagine: What if the inmate's actions might be better understood as the overcoming of one of these barriers, rather than the imperative to be kind, or decent? Violence might be an addiction for him, or something that he indulges in when he feels timid or powerless, or in order to overcome some deep disgust at violence itself, or at himself. If so, the counselor would need to bracket his desire to think that the *crucial* distinction is between moral and immoral actions, to understand why the inmate really did what he did. Counseling the inmate as if the barrier he had overcome was civility or the prohibition against stereotyping or violence won't help much at all.

In this way, Morton argues, our need to get a more immediate, superficial sharing, and to feel good about ourselves as a result, protects us from recognizing our deeper and more threatening sharing, a more terrifying similarity: we've done things more like the murderer than we can bear.

It's not a crass relativism, Morton's idea; his point is not that morality and ethics are, or should be, relative to our situation. He is outlining the limitations our fetishizing of empathy causes: the way protecting our image as a moral person can keep us from being exactly who we want to be—good at understanding the world and others, at preventing atrocities, at helping people to heal and change. He's also suggesting *why* we do this: in everyday life, in order to get along quickly with others, we need clear distinctions between moral and atrocious acts, without the kind of extensive knowledge of their contexts that it takes to really and deeply understand. And when we begin questioning the centrality and accuracy of our own perspective, searching out the details that matter so we can get a more accurate representation of the other, we find too much similarity, that too many "ordinary actions are continuous with many atrocious ones," and we can't function.

It is easier to choose to see others as mirrored inversions of our false sense of decency—to imagine that when they do selfish or violent things, it must be decency they abhor. When it speaks through us, sometimes, the narcissism script helps us do this, valorizing closeness and empathy as the ultimate moral good, and as what is increasingly lacking in others, so we can perform astonishment at the boyfriend, Milgram's subjects, the Nazis, the millennials, the world—in exactly that moment when, if we were to acknowledge the difference in context, we might find too threatening a similarity.

In the case of the bad boyfriend, the millennial, and the murderer, it's not just decency that keeps us from being able to actually understand and feel the other, but our beliefs about the opposition between human and inhuman, and our beliefs about mental "health." In fact, the mistake the script repeats and repeats—that what is human is the opposite of what is inhuman—may be partly responsible for keeping us, for centuries, from this deeper understanding of what it actually means to do what Morton calls "empathy's work."

The narcissism of decency, then, does exactly what we decent people fear: it prevents a deep sharing of feeling. But that sharing is the very feeling of being alive, and somewhere on the other side of our everyday moralizing, it is always there.

•

In a lab in Parma, Italy, in the early 1990s, neuroscientists noticed that inside the brains of macaque monkeys, the same neurons lit up when watching someone perform an action as they did when they performed the action themselves. These neurons came to be called mirror neurons, and sparked one of neuroscience's most remarkable recent revolutions. Housed in the ventral premotor cortex (area F5) and the inferior parietal lobule (area PF), mirror neurons, some argue, show how we understand, imitate, learn, and enjoy what others are doing: it is by actually simulating that action, doing it ourselves virtually, in our brains.

Mirror neurons may explain what primatologists like Frances de Waal have been arguing for a while now: our nearest primate relatives console one another, stop fights, create and follow social rules that make things more fair for one another, and return favors—all empathetic acts, and the building blocks of an uncannily human morality. It is rare that neuroscientists can implant sensors in the brains of humans, but some studies with epileptics, and neuroimaging in other cohorts, have hypothesized a similar mirror neuron circuit in the brains of humans. Subsequent studies have shown that as infants, we begin imitating our caretakers a few minutes after we're born, and that it may be mirror neurons that help us to learn language at such great speed, catch the emotions of others, and simulate their facial movements. The mirror neuron research deepens what we know from developmental psychology and findings in emotional contagion: we grow up to be people by simulating the actions of those near us. We simulate the World Cup goal even though it is the action of another. They seem to be susceptible to training, these mirror neurons—we simulate the goal more intensely if we have ever played soccer—but we all simulate it. We understand what others are doing, in other words, because we are doing inside ourselves what they do, whether we want to or not, whether we are conscious of it or not.

When the mirror neuron researcher V. S. Ramachandran announced the new "Neurology of Self-Awareness" in *Edge* in 2007, he celebrated the discovery as inherently spiritual, naming mirror neurons "empathy neurons" and "Dalai Lama neurons" because of the way in which, in the act of empathic mirroring, they "dissolv[e] the barrier between self and others." The discovery of mirror neurons confirms the suspicions of philosophers who have argued, against Kant's elegant formulation, that our ability to be kind and just and good arises not from careful reasoning but from our natural ability to know what others feel. When the word *empathy* made its way into English from the German *Einfühlung*, it meant "feeling into"—an ability that had been celebrated by philosophers in the tradition of Adam Smith and David Hume, and later, on the continental side, by phenomenologists such as Husserl and Heidegger. As long ago as 1759, in an oft-quoted passage, Smith wrote:

> Though our brother is upon the rack . . . By the imagination we place ourselves in his situation, we conceive ourselves enduring all the same torments, we enter as it were into his body, and become in some measure the same person with him, and thence form some idea of his sensations, and even feel something which, though weaker in degree, is not altogether unlike them.

In the two decades before the discovery of mirror neurons, Girard, like Hume, Smith, and the aesthetician Theodor Lipps, argued that we imitate others inside ourselves. This mimesis, he claimed throughout his work, is not only the primary way that we encounter and understand others, but how we come to be selves in the first place. The mirror neuron research is controversial and still unfolding, but it may confirm his suspicions: we are not born at the center of the world, but into a place somewhere between ourselves and our caretakers. We become selves only by mirroring in ourselves the actions of others, who we want to be like. We are, in this very real, material way, made of each other, and so we exist, Girard argued, not alone, boundaries secured, working out economic exchanges between ourselves and those who we might dare to love, but always somewhere in-between.

This was Girard's argument with Freud in the first place: in Freud's view, love was scarce, a forfeiting of oneself, a sacrifice, because we are all discrete and opposed to one another. Picturing the self that way is how you get to the idea of a narcissist who hoards affection, young people who hoard goods and attention, the narcisphere's stories about the narc and narc-feeder. But Girard, like Kohut and Winnecott before him, imagined that this imitation grows rather than diminishes the self.

It seems a comfort, the idea of all this sharing. But if we're as fluidly made as Girard says, our separateness is as much a mask as any cold villain's. While "dissolving the barrier between self and others" sounds lovely in a vaguely spiritual sense, Girard argued that it can also be the greatest threat, especially because we do not realize how much we are made of others, and we very definitely do not want to. And this unconscious fellow feeling is perhaps why it is so difficult, sometimes, for us to do what Morton suggests.

That the very ubiquity of imitation causes problems is confirmed by emotional contagion researchers:

> People seem to be capable of mimicking others' facial, vocal, and postural expressions with stunning rapidity. As a consequence, they are able to feel themselves into those other emotional lives to a surprising extent. And yet, puzzlingly, most people seem oblivious to the importance of mimicry and synchrony in social encounters. They seem unaware of how swiftly and how completely they are able to track the expressive behaviors and emotions of others.

Mimicry is so common, they continue, that the real variable that has the most effect is its lack: we are surprised and react strongly when we are *not* imitated. We freak out when the fellow feeling shuts down, partly because we do not realize, most of the time, when we're expressing it. And perhaps for good reason; sometimes, when we are on the verge of glimpsing it, it's the worst thing.

When you see the faces of your best friends, the same neurons light up that fire when you look at your own reflection. But if you reach for the same thing as a friend does, if you even unconsciously imitate his desires, and especially if you find yourself, despite yourself, attracted to his girlfriend, you have a problem. This was Girard's central insight: violence comes from imitation, from too much sameness, rather than too much difference. If we make ourselves out of one another, we also hide this at all costs. Our mimetic desires expose the mask, and when it tears,

Girard argues, violence is born: in the split second when it would be revealed that we are naught but the imitation of others, when we reach for what they want because we cannot help it, our whole neurological apparatus is on the verge of being laid bare. On just the other side of the comfort of fellow feeling, then, is war.

•

On a larger scale, the same thing that helps us understand accurately those close to us can prevent us from understanding the world at all. At the level of basic recognition, as in "recognizing that others are in the category of beings I care about," every organism has a limit. When macaques are shown pictures of other monkeys whose faces are like theirs, and then monkeys whose faces are less and less like theirs, they hit, somewhere along the way, what neuroscientists call the "uncanny valley," and freak out, just as we do.

Chickens, it has been demonstrated, can recognize and remember the individual faces of one hundred and ten other chickens. Beyond that, they seem bewildered, and panic. This is one reason why, when they're put in cages with hundreds or thousands of other chickens, they try to peck each other to death.

Splitting, the attempt to control the world by dividing it clearly into good and bad, is what a narcissist does when he turns cold, and why he's so scary: he's decided you're evil, or no longer in the realm of people who are with him, who feed his self-image, and therefore you are against him. But for chickens and monkeys and the rest of us, splitting happens, too, at the edge of our empathy scale, which is to say, the edge of the category of beings we recognize as familiar.

Studies show that because we have no idea how much of our knowledge about others comes from mirroring on the most local level, we project onto larger groups exactly our own levels of happiness, experience of crime, ability to solve problems, and political views, and the bigger the scale shift, the more wrong we tend to be.

De Waal worries that empathy for strangers, at greater scales, is so difficult for humans precisely because empathic accuracy evolved as a way of protecting one's in-group against outsiders and therefore does not extend to those outside one's group. Empathy evolved to make social organization stick together and last; in order to get along with some small group of other organisms, you must understand one another. If you're a herd animal, and prey, you need to be able to understand together in a split second what to do: you mirror the other alpacas, not the wolves, and you run.

At this point, the Internet bubbles creepily up at the edge of our view, above and below and all around us just beyond perception, glimpsed only briefly through the peephole of the screens of our devices, not some "superspreader" of individual narcissism, but a laboratory testing for empathy, even basic intraspecies recognition, at a scale and speed beyond which we have ever been capable.

•

The discovery of mirror neurons complicates the moralistic view of empathy underlying the prophecies of a narcissism epidemic; if understanding what others are doing and what they want is a function so basic as to be the very substrate of our lives, and of the lives of primates in general, it is not exactly the sine qua non of being good, on the one hand, or even of being human. And the relation of inner mirroring to being good, and unselfish, turns out to be tremendously complicated. We know more than ever and still it's less than clear when and how our empathy is accurate, and when it leads us to treat one another well. Lab studies of "empathic accuracy" try to untangle the first knot—how good are we at "feeling into" rather than just projecting?—by testing viewers' explanations of the emotions of another subject (in person or on video) against the self-reported emotional states of the person being observed. A test called Reading the Mind in the Eyes evaluates the ability to develop an accurate theory of mind about others. Researchers have found, for example, that autistic and Asperger's subjects are more mind-blind and that men are more autistic than women; people with borderline personality disorder are particularly hard for others to understand; abusive husbands tend to interpret their wives as critical and rejecting to an inaccurate extent, not because they don't have the capacity to mirror them but because they shut down their ability to understand what their wives are feeling. Longtime friends have better empathic accuracy than strangers, but for married couples, after a year, empathic accuracy declines.

And if neuroscience leaves us in a confusing place when it comes to understanding what kind of mirroring, what kind of sharing, leads to "prosocial" action, this is even more so the case with those called narcissists. There is one study showing that people who score high on the NPI don't automatically mirror others as much and therefore understand less about others. Yet empathic accuracy is something even sociopaths have, as well as people diagnosed with NPD. Before Tucker Max recanted his narcissism, Scott Barry Kaufman, who is a cognitive scientist at NYU, tested Max with the NPI (he scored 31/40), and then gave him the Reading the Mind in the Eyes test; Max also scored quite high—he was able to tell with remarkable accuracy what others were feeling. But on the Big Five personality test he scored predictably low on compassion. The problem may be that people can be very good at assessing the mental states of others without being conscious of sharing those states, as Kaufman argued in a *Huffington Post* article; awareness of sharing another's mental state is what motivates compassion. In this regard, some researchers make a distinction between warm and cold empathy. Yet others argue that it is precisely because people with NPD *do* share others' emotions, too much so, while being unable to distinguish between self and other, that those who test as narcissists turn cold with rage. Either way, Max's problem seems not to be a lack of understanding of others, as the narciscript claims, but the problem of the Girardan self, built through mirroring, only perhaps worse: just because we're made of sharing doesn't mean our understanding of others, often unconscious, leads us to care about them or treat them well.

Neuroscientists will continue to try to untangle these knots. But already, their findings trouble the script's view of narcissism as lack of empathy. They blur the difference between natural empathy and unnatural performance. They teach us that it is not just narcissists but all of us who create ourselves through unconscious and conscious mirroring and hide those reactions behind a mask of individuality. Our unconscious mirroring of others leads us to be more accurate in some situations, and less accurate in others, in our evaluations of what others are feeling. They confirm Girard's concern that mirroring is so omnipresent and unconscious that it can divide us.

We need to ignore all this, to support our idea that, because we're good, empathy with good people is easy, and empathy with bad people is hard. We need, Morton argues, to

> exaggerate the ease with which we can get accurate, non-pseudo, empathy in ordinary cases. We take it that any fellow-feeling that does not actually interfere with shared activity can be taken to represent real and significant psychological factors. And we minimize the ease with which we can make continuities with atrocious acts.

Maybe we do so especially when we believe (because all our conventional narratives of romance and friendship and mental health and intimacy tell us so) that someone should be for us the most familiar person in the world. The irony is that the kind of empathy that many women who believe themselves to be hooked up with narcissists describe themselves as having (calling themselves in contrast to their narcissist an "empath," a "clairvoyant," a highly sensitive person) then gets in the way of their understanding the narc at all. And at the other end of the scale, perhaps we are inclined to exaggerate our empathetic abilities when we confront strangers at the pace of the Internet.

But if the Internet is a laboratory testing for empathy, it is also our own deep, still reflecting pool. We see contagion daily on our screens, like the contagiousness of the emotions, thoughts, and small violences that constitute our very selves, dependent, contingent, empty, unnatural, mirrored, and made.

Girard calls it a "sacrificial crisis," when everything we try to keep different is revealed as too much the same. And so the fake and empty are on the altar, and every time we sacrifice them, we get to join the empathetic "us."

The ritual chorus: the culture is our bad boyfriend; the world is the murderer; and there are humans and beasts, empaths and vampires, depths and surfaces, warm, healthy selves and cold, empty, calculating ones, the good and the young, love and usefulness, other-regard and self-regard, authenticity and performance, the caring past and the shallow, cruel future, the sheep and the goats. What would it look like, instead, the empathy that actually "does empathy's work"?

•

Another story: a few years ago, four friends were sleeping in a little house on the island of Vieques, just off mainland Puerto Rico. As morning broke, each one of the friends woke in her separate room because of a strange feeling, an

important fullness in the silence. They did not know that
the others had woken, too. One by one, each went to her
own window, and found the house surrounded by a herd
of wild horses, their smooth and muscular bodies in a
kind of group repose, felt before they were apprehended.
In that half-awake moment, the friends each felt what
passes among beings simply from being bodily near. Who
is to say that these friends did not then experience something of what horses feel? But was it then, or in the tellings
and retellings of the tale in the morning, that they began
to understand the presence of the herd of horses as be-
nevolent? And if it was in the retellings, does that make
that joy less real, for being fiction and, at the same time,
interpretation?

To understand the selfishness of others, even a philosopher such as Morton must tell stories, tentative, specula-
tive ways to imagine ourselves out from our own position
stuck in space and time, unconscious of how much we're
looking in the mirror. The stories are multiple, to keep us
from knowing, for a while.

Part of Girard's argument, always, was that novelists
are best equipped to see through the "narcissistic illusion."
His critique of Freud is also a reading of Marcel Proust,
who depicted his protagonists' love objects—Marcel's
great obsession, Albertine, for example—much as Freud
depicted his female narcissists, as full of self-sufficiency
and what Freud called "blissful autonomy." According to
Girard, Proust dissolves the narcissistic illusion, imagining his way to the point where he no longer believes that
the other can be magical and, like other novelists Girard

wrote about throughout his career, does not conceal real being, as Plato feared, but actually pulls back the curtain on it.

If Proust is able to pull away the veil of the narcissistic illusion, perhaps it is because he, like any novelist, like Morton, can activate our mirroring, but then slow us down, help us see from more than one position at the same time, move us outward from the center of the world, where we're stuck, to a kind of categorical empathy, a sympathetic imperative, embodied and interpreted—like waking among a herd of wild horses at the break of day.

But then the empathy that would matter, which actually "does empathy's work," would not be the natural, human, authentic, unmediated feeling that the narcissism script gives its hero-victims, but something more like the thing for which its villains have often been condemned: Morton's word for it is *representation*, the felt virtuality of fiction and even memoir, of stories, like the one that started it all.

The Artist

Narcissus was born of rape to a nymph, Liriope. She was raped in a brook by Cephissus, the river god—she nearly drowned—and then the pretty nymph gave birth to an even prettier child, a child so charming that "even as a baby he inspired girls with thoughts of love." Liriope went to Tiresias, a prophet, to ask if her son would live a long life, and Tiresias said, "Only if he never comes to know himself."

Narcissus becomes a hunter. Both boys and girls adore him, but he never loves any back. One of the boys he has spurned, "love-sick and left behind," calls out to heaven to curse Narcissus: "O may he love himself alone," he cries, "and yet fail in that great love." And who should hear him but Nemesis, the god of revenge.

One day, when Narcissus is hunting deer in the forest, Nemesis serves a revenge that, in the last century, has become our story about coldness and self-love. But the prophecy was not that Narcissus would love himself, but that he would *know* himself; the curse was not that he would love himself, but that he would fail "in that great love."

•

Deep in the woods, Narcissus finds a dark pool, so solitary that not even birds visit it, writes Ovid, not even leaves fall on it. It is not even lit by the sun. Narcissus finds this pool "charming." Everyone is always throwing themselves at him; here, he can finally be alone.

But he does not think he is alone. In the pool, Narcissus catches a glimpse of his reflection. It is not that he gazes upon himself and likes what he sees; he makes a mistake, and thinks he sees someone else. He does not know that the qualities he finds in the image are his, the "two stars that were his eyes," the hair "divine as Bacchus' hair, as bright Apollo's," the "boyish beauty." He isn't cold; he wants to share emotion, and he thinks he and this other boy do, perfectly—"even as / I reach, your arms almost embrace me, and as / I smile, you smile again at me." He weeps, and the boy in the pool weeps, too, in perfect but virtual synchronicity. Because he thinks he is seeing another, he is frustrated when he cannot draw close, cannot hold the boy, and in grief, he gets stuck. He shouts into the forest in heartbroken confusion at the illusion of intimacy. It is the illusion that love could be this perfectly full, two identical people in such ideal harmony, a closed circuit, that Ovid gently tears apart, putting on Narcissus's tongue the lesson he would have us learn about the kind of love that mistakes one's own image for someone else:

Look! I am he; I've loved within the shadow
Of what I am, and in that love I burn,
I light the flames and feel their fires within;
Then what am I to do? Am I the lover
Or beloved? Then why make love? Since I
Am what I long for, then my riches are
So great they make me poor.

Narcissus reaches toward the boy he loves, and troubles
the water. The mask that he has made threatens to slip,
and he empties—"And now love drains / My life, look! I
am dying at life's primes." His tears disrupt the image,
and when the other boy ripples, looks strange, begins to
disappear, now Narcissus cries out for him not to leave.
He rips his clothes and beats his chest until it is purple
with bruises. Once cherry-cheeked and the picture of ado-
lescent vitality, he empties, turns pale, and fades away.

To mourn the absence of affection in someone, to
translate their turning away into emptiness, to mistake
your own emptiness for theirs, when desire simply makes
you feel this way: this is the tragedy Ovid gives us. Is Narcissus the cold, vain beloved, or a portrait of the victim?
Ovid has the boy ask us this himself: Is he the lover, or beloved? But in case we don't get it, Ovid's story is not only
about Narcissus.

To his likely source text, by Parthenius of Nicaea, Ovid
added a girl, Echo, who is also cursed. She can only repeat
what others say. Wandering in the forest, she catches sight
of Narcissus while he is out hunting, and just as fast as he

will for the boy in the pool, she falls immediately and ter-
ribly in love, like "sulphur / At the tip of torches, leaping
to fire / When another flame leans toward it." Burning like
that, she glides along in the forest beside Narcissus, wait-
ing for him to say the right words to the deer he is hunting,
so she can hunt him, too: *Come. Why run from me? Here
we shall meet.*

Poor Echo; she has no game. After a while, she comes
up with this brilliant strategy: she slips out from behind
a tree and throws her arms around Narcissus. Having
never met her before, his response is, understandably, fear:
"No, you must not touch—Go, take your hands away, may
I be dead / Before you throw your fearful chains around
me." Echo repeats, "O fearful chains around me." He gets
away from her, finds the pool, but remains in the woods
watching, distraught, repeating his sad words until he
wastes away entirely and turns into a flower, while his soul
heads to Hades.

•

There always come times when you see the story from
Echo's point of view, watching the one you want turn
away. He may be looking at someone else, but from the
perspective of Echo, he's looking at himself.

Maybe you catch a glimpse; maybe you catch him. It
could be her, or him, but let's go with him. Or maybe he
just starts withdrawing, doesn't even care enough to text
you where he is, and in the meantime, you've imagined
it, so precisely: he goes into a bar to meet her, a little early,
looks down at his phone when she texts that she's just

gotten off the train, texts "Run," like he used to text you. You are at home catching up on emails, maybe putting the baby to sleep, but you can see her, or imagine her, anyway, lit up on the sidewalk, fixing her makeup by checking her reflection in a store window, opening the door to the bar. She sees him down the bar, his face turned away, his body bent toward someone on the other side of him, and hesitates. But he knows she's there. He turns, sees her, and despite himself—and it is the *despite himself* that will get you, if you see it, or when you imagine it—his face lights up. He pushes up his left shirtsleeve and visibly tries to prevent a smile. He nods at her and pulls the empty barstool beside him close for her. It is not the way he kisses her, more hungrily than he has kissed you for months. It's not the difference that freaks you out. It's the similarity. The way he makes the familiar movements, smiles the same way, charmingly nervous, and yet everything he's doing seems responsive, singular, particular, about this one moment, this one girl.

But you can see, from your position, that it's not even about her, it's all about him. It's not just his absence that kills you, his abandonment, but the way it makes him turn strange, turns the most natural things into performances, fakes. If he can smile the same smile in response to what she is saying, if he can move his hands over her body in the same way he used to move his hands over your body, what he does must not be real, either not real with you, or not real with her, or both. And yet it feels so real; he feels, he has felt, so close. If he's capable of performing the movements of love—what kind of person can do this?— capable of faking affection, even nervousness, the pleasured glow, he must be empty of empathy. If he's not, if he is capable of empathy, he has shut it down when it comes to you, because you are not lovable anymore, or were never an end in yourself (how did you miss it?) but always a means, an object, an inhuman thing, empty.

·

In the Greek, *apocalypse* means a tearing away of a veil to reveal the truth. We've made a shorthand of it: violent cataclysm, the end of the world, as if the real truth will always be a disaster. His turning away is this: it rips the world as you knew it apart to show how close the end is, how replaceable you are, to reveal your unlivable fragility.

·

In Gay Talese's book *Thy Neighbor's Wife*, he reports that in open marriage groups in 1970s Los Angeles, sometimes, upon the first time a husband or wife would go to another room to be with someone else, their left-behind spouse would lose control and wail. Even though the spouse had chosen to participate in this scene, he or she would shake and even scream, like a small child torn from a parent, crying Echo's tears.

·

The narcissism script tells a story about a person who seems numb, and who, like the ancient flower that shares his name, can poison. But the script numbs, too. To the tragic situation, the apocalypse when you recognize your existence is inseparable from desire and can be wrecked by it, the script comes to the rescue, a prescription for a pain reliever.

·

Such inadequate comfort—deciding the bad boyfriend is evil—is better than suffering that apocalypse. It's better than feeling history leaving you behind: a generation or two of people who live half online, performing their minor celebrity in images and minimemoirs, looking for all the world as if they are only looking at themselves, uninterested in us, the future.

·

The script is univocal, turning every possibility into one, uncanny story: the others are fake, and you are real. But in Ovid's telling, it is much harder to get a bead on Narcissus; who he is depends on the position from which you view him.

Scholars speculate that from the perspective of Ovid's likely source, Parthenius, the story of Narcissus wasn't a condemnation of homosexuality; quite the contrary, it was a cautionary tale older men told to younger men they wanted to fuck, a warning, like our current prophecies about millennials, about vanity, an assertion of moral power. But from Freud's perspective, the tale becomes a story about queerness, the immature feminine, excess similarity, the refusal of mature, straight love, the script.

For Tiresias, the prophet, Narcissus's story is a cautionary tale about "knowing oneself," the illusions we fall into when we find ourselves everywhere. For Nemesis, Narcissus is just another bastard god-child to curse, the dumb and empty opposite, the boomerang of revenge. For Echo, he is what someone looks like when he has turned away, the nightmare of desire seen from an outside point of view, as total self-absorption.

Ovid's happiest love story is that of Baucis and Philemon. Their love is characterized by their hospitality and generosity to others. They are poor, but open their home to strangers despite their poverty, and in one case, the strangers turn out to be gods. When the gods want to reward them, their wish is that neither of them will die before the other. In fact, they do not die, but transform into two trees, a linden and an oak, that grow into one another from their separate root systems, their branches entwined, and they live in this way forever.

That is a kind of togetherness of which Narcissus and Echo can only dream, but they try so hard, it's almost funny. In comparison to Ovid's story of true love—hospitality to others, to the divine, twoness and oneness at the same time, and endless time—the original narcissism script looks less like a portrayal of pathology or evil and more a case of mistaken identities, the illusions we pass through on the way to love. Narcissus does not realize he is looking at his own face; he thinks he is looking at someone else. Echo, who does not have her own words but must live off the words of another, mistakes control and capture for love. Echo has no substance but the other; Narcissus's other has no substance but himself. From this perspective, their story is not about a narcissist, but Girard's "narcissistic illusion": the way we are made of each other, and don't know it. By adding Echo, and putting us in the woods watching them both, Ovid shows us the narc and victim as interchangeable, stuck in one place together, unable to see beyond the time they're in or even who's who—a spoof of the kind of togetherness Baucis and Philemon get by opening their home to those who they do not yet know are gods.

•

It is something you'll come to months or years later, if at all: the possibility that the way he was with you was real, and that it was love; that the way he was with the other woman, real or imagined, was real, was love, as well. You might understand this in the middle of the next time you fall in love with someone else, and find yourself, still, in love with him. You've just spread your love out in time, and he has spread it out in space.

But that is exactly what you can't get to, the perspective of time, when your gaze is frozen on the image of him turning away. You're suffering from the same illusion as both Echo and Narcissus: only one person can be the center of another person's world at any given time, and ideally, this would always be you. This is where all the narcissistic romance websites invite you to be: in the center of the world, stuck in time, assessing the moral status of others, until love is gone.

Long before Freud's narcissists, Ovid told us a story that was only partly about the dangers of vanity. It was also about the dangers of locking yourself in lament, gazing on one who is turning away, thinking she or he is so different from you, stuck in a moment you'll repeat forever, and mistaking that moment, from your perspective, for knowledge.

Devastated by a young man she has never spoken to, and who she fell for in a moment, Echo is destined to wander the forest for the rest of her life, eaten away by sorrow, until she becomes a "pale and wrinkled" shade, then a "sheet of air," then mere bones, which turn to "thin-worn rocks." Finally, she disappears until all that is left is her voice, repeating what others say. Even after Narcissus beats himself purple and turns from human into the flower that numbs, Echo's voice lasts, Ovid tells us: "She's heard by all who call; her voice has life."

Ovid sends Narcissus to the underworld but leaves us in the forest with Echo, repeating eternally the words that others say: oh, the selfishness of others, the selfishness, the selfishness.

The World

At some point, since surveys that measure the new selfishness—such as the NPI, upon which the prophecies of a narcissism epidemic are based—are unreliable, Twenge and Campbell began counting words. The words used in cultural products like novels and songs, they argued, are free of "the biases that plague self-report measures." Writing "I" clearly corresponds to self-centeredness, and writing "we" corresponds to other-centeredness. They found what they were looking for—since 1960, there's been a 10 percent decrease in the use of *us* and *we* in American novels and nonfiction, and a 42 percent increase in *I* and *me*. They also found that the use of *you* and *your* has quadrupled, but rather than seeing this as evidence of other-focus, or a symptom of an increase in the publication of psychological self-help books, they took this "increased tendency to directly address the reader and include him or her in the dialogue" to be "another indicator of individualism."

Like most scientists, the authors do write *we* rather than *I*, but then again, there are two of them, writing together.

This writer is hunched over her computer in a dark, high-walled room, alone, forehead creased at the study on her screen, thinking of "self-centered" sentences like *I'm sorry* and *I love you* and *Let me help* and *I wonder*. The writer is thinking, too, of that study—this is the last one—by Gebauer, Sedikides, Verplanken, and Maio, which found that "communal narcissists" attempt to satisfy narcissistic needs by being obviously generous and politically engaged, and by emphasizing their care for others. She is worrying over the fact that if attempting to perform empathy, compassion, and sociality can all be symptoms of a pathological need to maintain one's selfiness, and if it's true that you might use *we* because you're vainly attached to presenting an image of collectivity—not to mention the possibility that, on the other hand, the 42 percent increase in the use of *I* might be a symptom of an increase in people taking responsibility for things—this word counting would be, in a word, fucked.

What's left is stories, and a myth that just feels true, though after a while it frays the mind, at least the mind of this writer, who is beginning to see patterns the writers of *The Narcissism Epidemic* certainly didn't intend: Lauren, who wrote "Feeling special is a great form of motivation"; the governor with the classical music CDs for babies; the preschool with the TV studio, and the preschool where three-year-olds sing about their specialness; Linda, who sees big houses everywhere; the person with too much water during the water ban: all these people lived in Atlanta or in nearby Athens, Georgia. It is young middle-class couples in "places like Dallas, *Atlanta*, and San Diego" (emphasis ours) who the authors report want "beautiful dark wood flooring" for their new houses, even if the upgrade costs $50,000.

The Narcissism Epidemic does cite several instances of narcissism in San Diego, where Twenge is from: besides the dark wood incident, the authors cite a San Diego State University junior who said, about her generation, "But we are special"; a number of MySpace pages by young San Diegans that mentioned things such as "I LOVE TO PARTY" and "My friends are better than yours"; also at San Diego State, three girls participating in an annual "Undie Run" who wore panties that read "Take My Photo" across their asses, and then did repeatedly have their photo taken.

But more of the anecdotes seem to cluster in and around Atlanta, where the other author of *The Narcissism Epidemic*, Keith Campbell, is from, and Tucker Max, and of course Allison, who tried to shut down Peachtree Street. So many of the book's stories about narcissists are from Atlanta that the city begins to look like some kind of ground zero of the epidemic, unless it's just that these are the ones this writer notices because she's done time on Peachtree Street, which is probably the most important street in Atlanta. It cuts from downtown Atlanta up and out to the suburbs, where it turns into Peachtree Road. The most important buildings in Atlanta are on Peachtree Street. Scarlett O'Hara lived on Peachtree Street, and all the parades go down it. It's so important that seventy-one other streets in Atlanta are named after Peachtree Street: Peachtree Walk, Peachtree Circle, Peachtree Drive, Peachtree Way, New Peachtree Road, Peachtree Battle Avenue, and so on. So that if you're sitting in the backseat of a late-nineties Pontiac Bonneville, being driven around the Atlanta suburbs so that your boyfriend—"romantic affiliate," he was calling himself, at the time—can spend time with his boyhood best friend, who works nights and has to pay his probation officer that afternoon, but who then spends the rest of the afternoon trying to hustle your boyfriend/affiliate into footing the bill for a Percocet prescription, which involves a visit to a doctor who will write a prescription for fifty dollars and whose strip mall office bears the sign YOUR FAMILY DOCTOR with the *F* in FAMILY hanging askew, and then having given up on getting your boyfriend/affiliate to agree to funding said prescription, basically kidnaps your boyfriend and you along on a trip to pick up said prescription, never stopping the car until he parks it at Kroger, where the prescription is not available in an hour as promised, or even an hour later—a delay spent at Hick'ry House eating BBQ and then the Taco Mac sports bar drinking Budweisers, but even so a delay that becomes to your whatever, affiliate, absolutely excruciating, and ends in another inexplicable drive around Atlanta during which he slides lower and lower into the passenger seat in front of you like a little boy trying to disappear under the dinner table, his right arm draped with fraudulent casualness over his head but his fingers clutching the headrest so hard they've gone completely white from lack of blood, because all of the many steps in this hustle and then finally the scrip-getting itself have involved a frenetic crisscrossing of the Atlanta suburbs, due to the fact that said boyfriend's best friend is in so much physical and psychic pain (slipped disc and experiencing so much inner emptiness, or high self-esteem, one or the other), that if he has to wait more than ten seconds in a traffic situation he will get angry at the assholes taking up the road and suddenly exit the highway and try a different route, and then do a U-turn and get back on the highway, to avoid the other traffic, and yet all of Atlanta is traffic, all of it is, all the time, so then what you will see, everywhere you go, is Peachtree, Peachtree, Peachtree, and you will not know if you have traveled anywhere at all, if you are seeing all the suburbs of Atlanta and all their Peachtrees, or if you are just circling round and round the same exact place, from which perspective it looks as if an emptiness is spreading from Atlanta out into the rest of the country and across the globe, unstoppable.

"Sometimes I saw so many big connections," Campbell wrote in an acknowledgments section, "that I thought the black helicopters would come and take me away."

Any book you write is its own asylum, but a book about narcissism is like the padded cell inside the asylum.

•

The winter I began reading about the epidemic, twenty-four winter storms hit the northeastern United States: Atlas, for whom holding the sky on his shoulders was a punishment; Boreus, god of freezing winds of the north; Hercules, the strongest god; Janus, from the Roman tradition, who looks back and ahead, the god of transitions; Maximus, which isn't actually the name of a god at all, just Latin for "greatest." That winter, I flew from New York to Seattle, and as I passed over Lake Michigan, I saw that it was frozen. I texted my brother, who lives in Grand Rapids: "Your lake is frozen. I know this because you live in a flyover state, and I literally just flew over you." He texted back: "We're aware." My Atlantan boyfriend/romantic affiliate would give me the weather report as I was getting dressed for work: "Tomorrow, blisteringly cold," he would say, interpreting the symbols on his iPhone and stroking his beard. "Wednesday, snow again, and soul-crushingly cold." Even the Atlantic was frozen, as far as you could see from shore. In my apartment, I'd curl up on the couch with my friend from San Diego and read the copy about the next incoming storm aloud, giggling at the verbs the weatherpeople chose: the storm will batter and roar, drop and pummel us. "Who names these things," she said, laughing, "with the names of gods?" On the streets, we hunched our shoulders, trying to make ourselves cold to the cold, with that kind of perseverance that passes among friends at a bar, strangers on the subway trains.

The answer to her question about who named last year's storms is that the names were chosen by students in a Latin class at a Bozeman, Montana, high school, at the request of the Weather Channel. "It's simply easier to communicate about a complex storm," someone from the Weather Channel was quoted as saying, "if it has a name."

•

A year has passed, and it's another cold winter, and if the storms have names, I don't know what they are. The man from Atlanta now calls himself a boyfriend, and has been stirring in the next room. For an hour or so there is the sound of breakfast being made at a leisurely Georgia pace. Then he opens the study door.

"Good morning," he says.

Good morning.

He picks up a copy of *Freud and Beyond*. "*Freud and Beyond*," he says. "That title makes me want to shoot myself in the head."

I work at home, producing "content," sitting in this room and reading the Internet and writing about it. In here it's just the computer, the table, the books, a circle of lamplight. He brings me a plate and sits in the armchair by my desk. As we eat, he tells me the news from space: last week, scientists found the astrophysical equivalent of stretch marks in the universe. The first definitive empirical proof of the Big Bang. This means that the theory of eternal inflation is most likely true, and we know, because we read astrophysical news to one another a lot lately, that this means that there may be multiple universes. The results will be questioned by other astrophysicists within months, but we don't know that yet. We shake our heads together in wonder at the thought that there might be multiple universes humming alongside one another, or even, as some astrophysicists have speculated, passing through each other.

Mainly we sit in one or two rooms, working every second we can. Within five years, someone on the Internet tells me, a third of Americans will likely do the same, free-lancing online, alone.

I email Allison, and within a few hours she sends her number. "My life," she says, "is an open book."

"A lot of my sweet sixteen," Allison tells me, "didn't have to do with me." It was her father's party—he'd planned it all, far in advance of being approached by MTV. When the camera crews came, there wasn't much to do, so "there was a lot of, sort of, reaching for material." The family pretended to plan, to shop, to talk to the party planner about an entrance parade. This was pretty obvious from the episode, I say, and she laughs. "Oh, good." She's not that concerned. For her, the day was about her dad. "Every little girl wants to be like her daddy in some way," she said, "and that was my way to be like him, to have a huge party."

The show made it seem as if it was the other way around, I point out, that she was a domineering teen and her parents were doing whatever she said. She agrees. "That's how they have to frame it. It's never like they force you to act a certain way," she says of the MTV crew, "or to do a certain thing, but there's a lot of, like, leading questions, like 'Oh, so you really want this party to be great, and you want your friends to have a really great time, right?' And you're like, 'Yeah.' And they're like, 'Can you repeat that back?' And you're like, 'Sure.' So it's not necessarily made up, but it's not things that you thought of on your own, at the same time."

I think of Milgram, of the MTV reality machine as social psychology lab, and ask her whether the pressure to do what they said was good television, to act like a celebrity for a day, made her willing to act in ways she otherwise wouldn't. She shrugs off the idea. She had been around celebrities her whole young life, and knew they were just people like us. "I just wanted my dad to have his party."

She was embarrassed by the show afterward. Watching it on television was the first time she realized she hates the sound of her own voice. By the time she got to college, she had left the show behind, and it rarely came up. When she met DeQuan at the University of Miami, it was a month before he found out, from someone else, "so that was interesting."

As they fell in love, they found themselves to be uncannily similar and different. They'd grown up in the same city, but she in Buckhead, the wealthiest neighborhood, and he in Stone Mountain, the toughest. He wasn't given the "tools he needed to succeed," and she was, but, she told me, "I always noticed the kids that weren't." In her small private high school, she'd grown tired of the same people, who always hung out with other private-school kids. In her view, in Atlanta "you're not divided by race, so much as by class." And hanging out with public-school kids, she noticed the way that some of them were "ignorant," not in the sense of unintelligent, but in that they had been kept ignorant. DeQuan had felt it, because of traveling for basketball, the way getting to another place helps you see your own better. She had seen it since she was five, when her family went to Jamaica. You have to get outside your place, she believes, to know who to be in the world. If you don't, you're stuck. How can you know what to strive for, she said, unless you've seen it?

Allison and DeQuan's foundation aims to give impoverished kids in Atlanta the "tools they need to succeed," which means, so far, school supplies, but Allison hopes for something bigger: getting them out of their neighborhood, to plays and musicals and museums, to get a sense of a bigger world, and to encounter art. It has been an obsession of hers since she was young, the one thing about her sweet sixteen that really felt like hers: the theme of her party was travel. When her father suggested the parade down Peachtree Street, she objected; she couldn't understand what a parade had to do with travel. But it was his party.

I ask her about the things she does—blogging, posting careful selfies of new outfits, performing her life online—that make millennials so mysterious and shallow seeming, and to those who are older, so vain. "I don't think you should call us more narcissistic," she says. "This is going to sound narcissistic, though—I think you should call us the caring generation. We care about more people."

This confuses me, until I realize that she means we care about more strangers. "Yeah," she continues. "We care about strangers. We care about the experiences of others, even if we'll never meet them. I care about the girl I don't know who's writing a blog about how she and her husband packed up, as newlyweds, and traveled the world," she says. "I want to read it; I'm glad she's sharing it. And maybe she wants to read my story, too." I ask her why she cares, and she says, "Because I think I can learn from her." She lives in a small world, she says; anyone she finds online, if she tells a friend, who tells another friend, that third person will know the first person, too. "We really are more connected," she says. "It's really hard to find someone who no one knows."

Once she gets her counseling degree, she'll work with couples. She was the little girl who was always pretending she was married, with an imaginary husband and dolls for children; she has always believed in family, wanted to understand how families work, and she thinks women her age don't value long-term commitments, marriage, enough.

The cameras couldn't show her future, any more than they showed that on her sixteenth birthday, it was only one lane of Peachtree's six that was shut down for five minutes for the MTV shoot, and it wasn't her idea at all.

·

On my desk is the first volume of a six-volume chronicle of the mundane details of the life of the Norwegian man Karl Ove Knausgaard. On the cover is a photograph of his eyes, gazing somberly at me, his furrowed brow. In the second volume, near the end, he explains why he did it, how he had lost faith in fiction, because it was everywhere, everything shaped like stories, even the news, everything on the Internet—how fake everything had become. And I search the shelf so I can read it now:

> I couldn't write like this, it wouldn't work, every single sentence was met with the thought: but you're just making this up. It has no value. Fictional writing has no value, documentary narrative has no value. The only genres I saw value in, which still conferred meaning, were diaries and essays, the types of literature that did not deal with narrative, that were not about anything, but just consisted of a voice,

the voice of your own personality, a life, a face, a
gaze you could meet. What is a work of art if not
the gaze of another person? Not directed above us,
nor beneath us, but at the same height as our own
gaze.

He furrows his brow at me, and I at him.

I wonder how different it is, what he assumes, from
what Allison so easily assumes, that because I want to read
your story, and meet your gaze, I tell mine, and when I do,
I am looking for you.

Transcribing the interview with Allison, I hate the
sound of my own voice, and it strikes me how strong hers
is, and how relaxed. I was born in the uncanny valley between the millennial generation and Generation X, at
home neither on the Internet nor in a world without it. But
she sounds at home. It makes me nervous—doesn't it you?—
and excited, too, to imagine, for a second, that everyone is
an artist, now, writing our memoirs all day long, finding
the real in the fake and the fake in the real, Plato be
damned, and that this is a good thing, that it's harder and
harder to find someone who no one knows.

•

Upstairs, in the apartment above us, a puppy is crying,
and I'm anxious. I walk out to find the man from Atlanta
in the kitchen. He's oddly vivid and shifting. A white man
with dirty blond hair, a beard, the trace of a Georgia
drawl. I know his eyes are green, but they look deep blue

when he wears blue, or opaque and luminescent silver when he wears brown, and because of the beard they are the main thing about his face. There are three distances in his eyes: near, middle, and far. The near distance glitters, and when he is drunk or high it is all near; from the middle distance, mostly veiled by the twinkling foreground, he watches everyone; the far distance is seldom visible, and very sad. Today it is all middle.

I ask him what will happen in the future. Usually he says, "I don't know." It's an old joke between us, that we play on repeat like a favorite song. But this time, he says he'll tell me when we're fifty.

I am older than he is, so I ask, "When I am fifty, or when you are?"

By that time, he says, we will have grown to be the same age.

"How?" I say.

He loves Vonnegut; he says, "We'll come unstuck in time."

The morning after the Peachtree hustle we woke in Athens, Georgia, three hours late to meet his parents at a Waffle House an hour away. That kind of moment when things have gone so wrong it seems you might be, finally, found out as a total asshole. "What are we gonna do?" I asked. He said the same thing. "We'll come unstuck in time."

"Vonnegut was talking," I say today, "about the psychic effects of trauma."

There's a sentence of Alice Miller's looping in my

mind, about grandiose people and depressives, Narcissus and Echo: "Neither can accept the truth that this loss or absence of love has already happened in the past, and that no effort whatsoever can change this fact." It's the main thing I've learned from reading all this psychology: the future is always trying to feel like the past. When it does, it feels like selfishness, hurt, loss at the hands of others. The trick is to let it empty. Maybe this is another way to come unstuck in time.

For years, whenever he turned away, I filled in the blanks with the script, but now he is here all the time, he won't leave, and even so close by, his mind—the other's mind—can turn strange and blank. You can fill in the blank with stories about coldness and stories of evil. You can try to chase it down, rope it, you can make war on it, but it will still be blank. You can rage against your dependency, the absolute need for the other that can never be satiated, but the other is, in their own way and not through their own fault, the very center of their universe, and there is a part of that centrality that will always be empty of you. You can study it and theorize it, but if the blank were not still bottomless, love would not ever go on long.

Maybe it's not something to run from, but one of the best things, the way no matter how hard we try to study them, the selves of others escape capture. It is something to turn toward, the selfishness of others, a kind of gift: the thing that can empty the future of your fears from the past.

The selfishness of others is the feeling of your dependence revealed, as their gaze turns away. Your independence laid bare as myth. The feeling of being the animal you are, born of other animals, made of mirroring them.

The selfishness of others is the feeling of time moving past you; what history feels like.

The selfishness of others is the feeling of the center shifting, the knowledge it was never under you. The feeling of living in physical space.

The doorknob of my apartment is loose because in the past I did not fix it, and unless I do, this doorknob will be broken in every future of mine, and in the future of the person who moves in next. Outside, a brownstoned and tree-lined block, gentrified Brooklyn. It is so cold, most of the sidewalks shoveled already, drift-lined, the sharp whir of a car spinning its tires. So cold that the Atlantic is frozen, just a couple miles away. But under the surface, the fish are swimming more slowly, the bluefish and fluke, bass, flying fish, and also jellyfish and sea turtles, the fin and minke whales, dolphins, and sharks, however many are left.

I've been inside and online, reading psychology and worrying over my intimates so long that pedestrians come toward me like enemy Galaga aliens plummeting down a screen. I am walking too slowly, and a man huffs his way around me from behind, "Goddammit, watch where you're going." There is a family taking up the sidewalk at the entrance to the subway, folding up a stroller and helping a small child down the first stair, and my own blood boils, my breath shortens, as I try to pass.

And then the feeling of physical space, the perspective of what is left behind, when we're locked in moral diagnosis.

Underneath this street is the second-biggest oil spill in American history. Every few weeks or months, a chemical smell in my building, and new construction at the end of the block. I drop a cigarette into a snowbank and it bores a hot hole into the snow and disappears. It's behind me, and in front of someone else.

The feeling of my selfishness is absence: the absence from my life of the trash I leave behind, which becomes the structures into which others must live, the broken hearts, the warmer air, the slower fish, the rising ocean: whatever I do not feel, that to others becomes the shape of their world.

My personal future smells like the past and looks like condos. It comes to me in the form of the explosion that began the universe, in the form of buildings on their way to ruin, the trash of the past, the refugees from the present's wars and poverties, the coming floods, the slow fish. But it is empty, so far, of feeling. It need not be full of selfishness, yet. There is time, still, to move backward into the future of others, gazing at the disasters we are leaving behind and trying to mend. My selfishness will be invisible until spring, when the world warms, the snow melts, and someone else turns the corner to find this littered street.

Narciphobia

A pervasive pattern of paranoia (in fantasy or behavior), splitting (organizing people, events, and the world into categories of good and evil, real and fake, deep and superficial, etc.), and catastrophizing, beginning by early adulthood and present in a variety of contexts, as indicated by five (or more) of the following:

1. Is preoccupied with the idea that he or she is surrounded by people who are trying to manipulate him or her for self-serving purposes.
2. Requires excessive reassurance that there are "real" people behind the avatars of others.
3. Has a tendency to spend large amounts of time in online "research" seeking diagnoses for romantic partners, family members, and sometimes complete strangers.
4. Is preoccupied with fantasies of "irl" relationships and opposes them to meaningful virtual forms of relating.
5. Believes that he or she is "special" and uniquely unselfish and can only be understood by, or should associate with, other people with low-selfishness scores.
6. Has a grandiose sense of empathy (e.g., exaggerates understanding of other people's motives and feelings beyond quantified empathy brain scan scores).

7. Lacks empathy: unusually quick to judge others based on superficial interactions; a tendency to sprint away in the middle of conversations with others.

8. Inconsistent cultivation of personal happiness resources, at the expense of freelance productivity/page views; often unable to swim to the occasional onsite meeting.

9. Inability to take responsibility for the floods; preoccupied with fantasies that the world is ending because of the selfishness of others.

—Proposed entry for the *Diagnostic and Statistical Manual of Mental Disorders,* Sixth Edition (2026)

Notes

THE COLD

3   *"My sweet sixteen"*: "Allison" from MTV's *My Super Sweet 16*, season 4, ep. 1, January 8, 2007. Also quoted in Jean M. Twenge and W. Keith Campbell, *The Narcissism Epidemic*. New York: Simon & Schuster, 2009; 101.

8   *"when the curtain falls"*: Alexander Lowen, quoted in "Narcissism." Wikipedia: accessed January 13, 2014.

9   *"What does one do"*: Tina Swithin, "8 Red Flags That You May Be Dating a Narcissist Like the One I Married." From *xojane*, December 18, 2012, www.xojane.com/sex/narcissists-should-come-with-warning-labels.

10   *"Like so many mental health professionals"*: Neil J. Lavender, "3 Key Tells That You're in a Relationship with a Narcissist." *Psychology Today*, August 22, 2013. www.psychologytoday.com/blog/impossible-please/201308/3-key-tells-youre-in-relationship-narcissist.

11   *American writers are using* I *and* me: Jean M. Twenge, W. Keith Campbell, and Brittany Gentile, "Changes in Pronoun Use in American Books and the Rise of Individualism, 1960–2008." *Journal of Cross-Cultural Psychology* 44, no. 3 (2012): 406–15.

THE EPIDEMIC

17 *"behavior that deviates markedly"*: American Psychiatric Association, *Diagnostic and Statistical Manual of Mental Disorders,* 5th ed. Washington, D.C., 2013; 645.

19 *"almost sociopathic narcissism"*: Twenge and Campbell, *Narcissism Epidemic*, 101.

19 *One in ten Americans*: Ibid., 2.

19 *"on that plane"*: Ibid., 56.

20 *"Twitter convinces them"*: Ike Awgu, "Edward Snowden Is No Hero," www.huffingtonpost.ca/ike-awgu/edward-snowden-narcissist_b_3484207.html.

26 *"My narc in-law"*: The examples in this paragraph are slightly fictionalized, to protect the privacy of posters, but representative.

28 *"cult following"* and *"recreating 'Narcissism'"*: Invicta, "Sam Vaknin Revisited," from www.friedgreentomatoes.org/articles/malignant_self_love.php.

29 *"This pattern, always adjacent to suffering"*: Catherine Keller, *Apocalypse Now and Then.* Boston: Beacon Press, 1996; 11.

29 *"We are in apocalypse"*: Ibid., 12.

THE BAD BOYFRIEND

32 *"We may 'do an apocalypse'"*: Keller, *Apocalypse*, 11.

33 *"The biggest mistake a lot of women make"*: Savannah Grey, "Are You Involved with a Broken Down? Understanding When It's Time to Fold 'Em," *Esteemology*, June 2013. http://esteemology.com/are-you-involved-with-a-broken-down-understanding-when-its-time-to-fold-em.

35 *"narcissism and homosexuality were fatally entwined"*: Elizabeth Lunbeck, *The Americanization of Narcissism.* Cambridge: Harvard University Press, 2014; 84.

35 *"the type of female most frequently met with"*: Sigmund Freud, "On Narcissism," in *Freud's On Narcissism*, edited by Joseph Sandler, Ethel Spector Person, and Peter Fonagy. New Haven, CT: Yale University Press, 1991; 18.

35 *Women, especially if they are beautiful*: Ibid., 18–19.

36 *"The charm of a child"*: Ibid., 19.

36   *"blissful state of mind"*: Ibid., 19.

36   *"inaccessible to the influence"*: Ibid., 4.

37   *"On the contrary, the patient sees"*: Sigmund Freud, *An Outline of Psycho-analysis,* in *The Standard Edition,* translated and edited by James Stachey. New York: W. W. Norton and Company, 1949; 52.

38   *"not due to any tendentious desire on my part"*: Freud, "On Narcissism," 19.

38   *"masculine lines"* and *"in the masculine way"*: Ibid., 20.

38   *"a part of their body"*: Ibid., 20.

39   *"We are quite ready to accuse others"*: René Girard, "Psycho-analytic Mythology," in *Things Hidden Since the Foundation of the World,* translated by Stephen Bann and Michael Metteer. Stanford: Stanford University Press, 1978; 391.

40   *"really taken in"*: René Girard, "The Narcissism Myth Demystified by Proust," in *Mimesis & Theory,* edited by Robert Doran. Stanford: Stanford University Press, 2008; 186.

41   *"two open ears and one temporal lobe lubricated"*: Quoted in Lunbeck, *Americanization of Narcissism,* 94.

42   *"out in the cold"*: Quoted in Lunbeck: Ibid., 92.

47   *"It would be wrong to believe"*: Girard, "Narcissism Myth," 183.

48   *The story of these arguments*: For a fuller account of the Kohut/Kernberg debate over narcissism, and of the history of psychology since Freud, see Lunbeck, *Americanization of Narcissism,* and Stephen A. Mitchell and Margaret J. Black, *Freud and Beyond: A History of Modern Psychoanalytic Thought.* New York: Basic Books, 1995.

51   *"If there's one thing I've learned"*: Heinz Kohut, *How Does Analysis Cure?* Chicago: University of Chicago Press, 1984; 93–94.

52   *"This disorder appears to be more common"*: American Psychiatric Association, *Diagnostic and Statistical Manual of Mental Disorders,* 3rd ed. Washington, D.C., 1979; 317.

53   *"It is a slippery slope"*: Strozier, *Heinz Kohut,* 314.

THE MILLENNIAL

62   *"almost sociopathic narcissism"*: Twenge and Campbell, *Narcissism Epidemic,* 101.

63   *"Even music and entertainment"*: Ibid., 60.

64   *"Every society reproduces its culture"*: Christopher Lasch, *The Culture of Narcissism: American Life in an Age of Diminishing Expectations.* 1979. Reprint, New York, W. W. Norton, 1991; 34.

64   *"Notwithstanding his occasional illusions"*: Ibid., 10.

76   *"feeling special is a great form"*: Twenge and Campbell, *Narcissism Epidemic*, 41.

76   *"if that's the definition of a narcissist"*: Ibid., 41.

76   *"I am special"*: Ibid., 16.

76   *"raised six children"*: Ibid., 131.

78   *"The social psychology of this century"*: Stanley Milgram, *Obedience to Authority: An Experimental View.* New York: Harper Perennial, 1974; 205.

79   *"The disappearance of a sense of responsibility"*: Ibid., 8.

79   *"smacks of dramaturgy or theatre"*: Milgram, quoted in Millard, 445.

79   *If administering shocks*: Ibid., 446.

84   *"special sensitivity to the unconscious signals"*: Alice Miller, *The Drama of the Gifted Child: The Search for the True Self*, translated by Ruth Ward. 1979. Reprint, New York: Penguin, 1997; 8–9.

84   *"Who else," writes Miller, "without this previous history"*: Ibid., 9.

86   *It is a private labor made increasingly public*: For a fuller account of the quantification of well-being, see William Davies, *The Happiness Industry.* London: Verso, 2015.

THE MURDERER

90   *"an almost indescribable manifestation"*: Quoted in "Anders Behring Breivik Complains of 'Inhumane Conditions' in Prison," *The Guardian*, November 9, 2012; www.theguardian.com/world/2012/nov/09/breivik-complains-inhumane-conditions-prison.

91   *"civilizational habit"* and *"numb complicity"*: Keller, *Apocalypse*, 8.

92   *A year after his experiment, researchers at Northwestern University*: Frances de Waal, "The Evolution of Empathy," *Greater Good*, September 1, 2005. http://greatergood.berkeley.edu/article/item/the_evolution_of_empathy.

92   *"One person, A, has empathy for another"*: Adam Morton, "Empathy for the Devil," in *Empathy: Philosophical and Psychological Perspectives*. Oxford: Oxford University Press, 2011; 319.

97   *"empathy's work"*: Ibid., 321.

97   *In a lab in Parma*: Marco Iacoboni, *Mirroring People: The Science of Empathy and How We Connect with Others*. New York: Farrar, Straus and Giroux, 2009.

99   *"Though our brother is upon the rack"*: Adam Smith, *Theory of Moral Sentiments*. Oxford: Clarendon Press, 1959/1976; 9.

101 *"People seem to be capable of mimicking"*: E. Hatfield, R. L. Rapson, and T. C. L. Le, "Emotional Contagion and Empathy," in *The Social Neuroscience of Empathy*, edited by Jean Decety and William Ickes. Cambridge/London: MIT Press, 2009; 26.

102 *When macaques are shown pictures*: Shawn A. Steckenfinger and Asif A. Ghazanfar, "Monkey Visual Behavior Falls into the Uncanny Valley." *PNAS* 106, no. 43 (October 27, 2009): 18362–66.

102 *Chickens, it has been demonstrated*: Carolynn L. Smith and Sarah L. Zielinski, "The Startling Intelligence of the Common Chicken." *Scientific American*, February 1, 2014; www.scientificamerican.com/article/the-startling-intelligence-of-the-common-chicken.

104 *And the relation of inner mirroring*: For a fuller explanation of the studies cited in this paragraph and the next, see the review essays compiled in Decety and Ickes, *Social Neuroscience of Empathy*. See also "Empathy," in the *Stanford Encyclopedia of Philosophy*.

104 *Researchers have found, for example, that*: Decety and Ickes, *Social Neuroscience of Empathy*, 57–70.

105 *Before Tucker Max recanted*: Scott Barry Kaufman, "Are Narcissists Better at Reading Minds?" *Huffington Post Science*, February 14, 2012; www.huffingtonpost.com/scott-barry-kaufman/narcissists-theory-of-mind_b_1279069.html.

105 *But already, their findings trouble*: "Empathy and Sympathy," from *The Internet Encyclopedia of Philosophy*, www.iep.utm.edu/emp-symp.

106 *"exaggerate the ease"*: Morton, *Empathy for the Devil*, 330.

THE ARTIST

111 *Narcissus was born of rape*: All quotes from Ovid, *The Metamorphoses,* translated by Horace Gregory. New York: Viking, 1958; 95–100.

116 *In Gay Talese's book* Thy Neighbor's Wife: Gay Talese, *Thy Neighbor's Wife,* 1980. Reprint, New York: Harper Perennial, 2009; 218–26.

THE WORLD

121 *"the biases that plague self-report measures"*: Twenge et al., "Changes in Pronoun Use," 407.

121 *"increased tendency to directly address the reader"*: Ibid., 412.

122 *which found that "communal narcissists"*: J. E. Gebauer, et al. "Communal Narcissism." *Journal of Personality and Social Psychology* 103, no. 5 (2012): 854–78.

122 *middle-class couples*: Twenge and Campbell, *Narcissism Epidemic,* 164.

123 *"But we are special"*: Ibid., 39.

123 *"I LOVE TO PARTY"*: Ibid., 115.

125 *"Sometimes I saw so many big connections"*: Ibid., 324.

131 *"I couldn't write like this"*: Karl Ove Knausgaard, *My Struggle: Book 2*, translated by Don Bartlett. New York: Farrar, Straus and Giroux, 2013; 562.

Selected Bibliography

For a complete list of studies consulted, see the author's website at
www.kristindombek.com.

American Psychiatric Association. *Diagnostic and Statistical Manual of Mental Disorders.* 3rd ed. (DSM-III). Washington, D.C., 1979.
———. *Diagnostic and Statistical Manual of Mental Disorders.* 5th ed. (DSM-V). Washington, D.C., 2014.
Baron-Cohen, Simon. *The Science of Evil: On Empathy and the Origins of Cruelty.* New York: Basic Books, 2011.
Decety, Jean, and William Ickes, eds. *The Social Neuroscience of Empathy.* Cambridge: MIT Press, 2009.
Freud, Sigmund. *An Outline of Psychoanalysis.* In *The Standard Edition.* Translated and edited by James Stachey. New York: W. W. Norton, 1949.
———. "On Narcissism: An Introduction." In *Freud's On Narcissism: An Introduction.* Edited by Joseph Sandler, Ethel Spector Person, and Peter Fonagy. New Haven: Yale University Press, 1991; 3–31.
———. "The Uncanny." In *The Standard Edition*, Volume XVII (1917–1919): *An Infantile Neurosis and Other Works.* Translated and edited by James Strachey. London: Hogarth Press, 1975; 217–56.

Gebauer, Jochen E., Constantine Sedikides, Bas Verplanken, and Gregory R. Maio. "Communal Narcissism." *Journal of Personality and Social Psychology*. 103, no. 5 (2012): 854–78.

Girard, René. "Narcissism: The Freudian Myth Demystified by Proust." *Mimesis & Theory,* edited by Robert Doran. Stanford: Stanford University Press, 2008; 175–93.

———. "Psychoanalytic Mythology." *Things Hidden Since the Foundation of the World*. Translated by Stephen Bann and Michael Metteer. Stanford: Stanford University Press, 1978.

Iacoboni, Marco. *Mirroring People: The Science of Empathy and How We Connect with Others*. New York: Farrar, Straus and Giroux, 2009.

Kant, Immanuel. *Grounding for the Metaphysics of Morals*. 1785. 3rd ed. Translated by James W. Ellington. Indianapolis, IN: Hackett, 1993.

Keller, Catherine. *Apocalypse Now and Then: A Feminist Guide to the End of the World*. Boston: Beacon Press, 1996.

Kernberg, Otto. *Borderline Conditions and Pathological Narcissism*. Lanham: Rowman and Littlefield, 1975.

Kohut, Heinz. *The Analysis of the Self: A Systematic Approach to the Psychoanalytic Treatment of Narcissistic Personality Disorders*. New York: International University Press, 1977.

———. *How Does Analysis Cure?* Chicago: University of Chicago Press, 1984.

———. *The Two Analyses of Mr. Z. The International Journal of Psychoanalysis* 60, no. 1 (1979): 3–27.

Lasch, Christopher. *The Culture of Narcissism: American Life in an Age of Diminishing Expectations*. 1979. Reprint, New York: W. W. Norton, 1991.

Lunbeck, Elizabeth. *The Americanization of Narcissism*. Cambridge: Harvard University Press, 2014.

Manne, Anne. *The Life of I: The New Culture of Narcissism*. Melbourne, Australia: Melbourne University Press, 2014.

Milgram, Stanley. *Obedience to Authority: An Experimental View*. New York: Harper Perennial, 1974.

Millard, Kathryn. "Revisiting Obedience: Exploring the Role of Milgram's Skills as a Filmmaker in Bringing His Shocking Narrative to Life." *Journal of Social Issues* 70, no. 3 (2014): 439–55.

Miller, Alice. *The Drama of the Gifted Child: The Search for the True Self.* Translated by Ruth Ward. 1979. Reprint, New York: Penguin, 1997.

Mitchell, Stephen A. and Margaret J. Black. *Freud and Beyond: A History of Modern Psychoanalytic Thought.* New York: Basic Books, 1995.

Morton, Adam. "Empathy for the Devil," in *Empathy: Philosophical and Psychological Perspectives.* Oxford: Oxford University Press, 2011. 318–30.

My Super Sweet 16. MTV, season 4, ep. 1 ("Allison"), January 8, 2007.

Ovid. *The Metamorphoses.* Translated by Horace Gregory. New York: Viking, 1958.

Strozier, Charles. *Heinz Kohut: The Making of a Psychoanalyst.* New York: Other Press, 2001.

Talese, Gay. *Thy Neighbor's Wife.* New York: Harper Perennial. 1980. Reprint, New York, Harper Perennial, 2009.

Twenge, Jean M., *Generation Me.* New York: Simon & Schuster, 2006.

Twenge, Jean M., and W. Keith Campbell. *The Narcissism Epidemic: Living in the Age of Entitlement.* New York: Simon & Schuster, 2009.

Twenge, Jean M., W. Keith Campbell, and Brittany Gentile. "Changes in Pronoun Use in American Books and the Rise of Individualism, 1960–2008." *Journal of Cross-Cultural Psychology* 44, no. 3 (2012): 406–15.

Acknowledgments

My gratitude to those who gave support and advice during this writing, including those who offered crucial responses to drafts: Nicole Callihan, Marion Wrenn, Svetlana Chirkova, Catherine Neckes, and Mel Flashman. My deep gratitude to Mel, my brilliant friend and agent, whose ideas and questions inspire me. I had the rare opportunity to work with not one but two extraordinary editors—Mitzi Angel, who invited me to write this essay, and Lorin Stein, who got me to finish it—from whom I have learned so much, and to whose rigorous understanding I am indebted. Thanks to John Knight and everyone at FSG who worked with patience and precision to get the book out. Thanks to the Rona Jaffe Foundation, to Dayna Tortorici and the *n+1* Foundation, and to the Imitatio Foundation for support during the writing. Thanks to Amanda Irwin Wilkins and everyone at my intellectual home, the Princeton Writing Program, and to the students who showed me that the prophets of the epidemic were wrong about them and the future. Heartfelt thanks to Allison Mathis Jones, who was gracious enough to represent a whole generation. When I'd been reading psychological studies and self-help websites for too many months, her warm voice on the telephone gave me hope. Without Stephanie K. Hopkins, this wouldn't have been written; for all you've taught me, thank you. To Dawn Lundy Martin, for how you think and live, thank you, and to both of you, for the fireplace, the picnic table, your writing to live by, my deepest thanks. And finally, thanks to William Martin, Jr.—for being my best friend and tough-minded encourager, my muse and home, for all you've done to get us through, and for the gift of your inimitable self, a lifetime of gratitude.